Shakespearean **Metaphysics**

Shakespeare

Series edited by Ewan Fernie and Simon Palfrey

Shakespearean Metaphysics

Michael Witmore

continuum

Continuum International Publishing Group

The Tower Building
11 York Road
London SE1 7NX

80 Maiden Lane, Suite 704
New York
NY 10038

www.continuumbooks.com

British Library Cataloguing-in-Publication Data
A catalogue record for this book is available from the British Library.

ISBN: 978-0-8264-9043-8 (hardback)
           978-0-8264-9044-5 (paperback)

Library of Congress Cataloging-in-Publication Data
A catalog record for this book is available from the Library of Congress.

Typeset by Newgen Imaging Systems (P) Ltd, Chennai, India
Printed and bound in Great Britain by Athenaeum Press Ltd, Gateshead, Tyne and Wear

For Silas

We often assume the impossible, so as to understand the nature of things in and of themselves.

— Johannes Philoponus (sixth century), *Commentary on Aristotle's* Physics

Contents

General Editors' Preface

Shakespeare Now! represents a new form for new approaches. Whereas academic writing is far too often ascendant and detached, attesting all too clearly to years of specialist training, *Shakespeare Now!* offers a series of intellectual adventure stories: animate with fresh and often exposed thinking, with ideas still heating in the mind.

This series of 'minigraphs' will thus help to bridge two yawning gaps in current public discourse. First, the gap between scholarly thinking and a public audience: the assumption of academics that they cannot speak to anyone but their peers unless they hopelessly dumb-down their work. Second, the gap between public audience and scholarly thinking: the assumption of regular playgoers, readers, or indeed actors that academics write about the plays at a level of abstraction or specialization that they cannot hope to understand.

But accessibility should not be mistaken for comfort or predictability. Impatience with scholarly obfuscation is usually accompanied by a basic impatience with anything but (supposed) common sense. What this effectively means is a distrust of really thinking, and a disdain for anything that might unsettle conventional assumptions, particularly through crossing or re-drafting formal, political or theoretical boundaries. We encourage such adventure, and base our claim to a broad audience upon it.

Here, then, is where our series is innovative: no compromising of the sorts of things that can be thought; a commitment to publishing powerful cutting-edge scholarship; *but* a conviction that these things are essentially communicable, that we can find a language that is enterprising, individual and shareable.

To achieve this we need a form that can capture the genuine challenge and vigour of thinking. Shakespeare is intellectually exciting, and so too are the ideas and debates that thinking about his work can provoke. But published scholarship often fails to communicate much of this. It is difficult to sustain excitement over the 80–120,000 words customary for a monograph: difficult enough for the writer, and perhaps even more so for the reader. Scholarly articles have likewise become a highly formalized mode not only of publication, but also of intellectual production. The brief length of articles means that a concept can be outlined, but its implications or application can rarely be tested in detail. The decline of sustained, exploratory attention to the singularity of a play's language, occasion or movement is one of the unfortunate results. Often 'the play' is somehow assumed, a known and given thing that is not really worth exploring. So we spend our time pursuing collateral contexts: criticism becomes a belated, historicizing footnote.

Important things have got lost; above all, any vivid sense as to why we are bothered with these things in the first place. Why read? Why go to plays? Why are they important? How does any pleasure they give relate to any of the things we labour to say about them? In many ways, literary criticism has forgotten affective and political immediacy. It has assumed a shared experience of the plays and then averted the gaze from any such experience, or any testing of it. We want a more ductile and sensitive mode of production; one that has more chance of capturing what people are really thinking and reading about, rather than what the pre-empting imperatives of journal or respectable monograph tend to encourage.

Furthermore, there is a vast world of intellectual possibility – from the past and present – that mainstream Shakespeare criticism has all but ignored. In recent years there has been a move away from 'theory' in literary studies: an aversion to its obscure jargon and complacent self-regard; a sense that its tricks were too easily rehearsed and that the whole game has become one of diminishing returns. This has further encouraged a retreat into the supposed safety of historicism. Of course the best such work is stimulating, revelatory and indispensable. But too often there is little trace of any struggle; little sense that the writer is coming at the subject afresh, searching for the most appropriate language or method. Alternatively, the prose is so laboured that all trace of an urgent story is quite lost.

We want to open up the sorts of thinking – and thinkers – that might help us get at what Shakespeare is doing or why Shakespeare matters. This might include psychology, cognitive science, theology, linguistics, phenomenology, metaphysics, ecology, history, political theory; it can mean other art forms such as music, sculpture, painting, dance; it can mean the critical writing itself becomes a creative act.

In sum, we want the minigraphs to recover what the Renaissance 'essay' form was originally meant to embody. It meant an 'assay' – a trial or a test of something; putting something to the proof; and doing so in a form that is not closed-off and that cannot be reduced to a system. We want to communicate intellectual activity at its most alive: when it is still exciting to the one doing it; when it is questing and open, just as Shakespeare is. Literary criticism – that is, really thinking about words in action, plays as action – can start making a much more creative and vigorous contribution to contemporary intellectual *life*.

Simon Palfrey
Ewan Fernie

Acknowledgements

This book was inspired by a footnote in Graham Harman's *Tool Being: Heidegger and the Metaphysics of Objects* and was nursed by conversations with Daniel Selcer, with whom I co-taught a graduate seminar entitled 'Late Epicureanism: Varieties of Materialism in Early Modernity' during the spring term of 2007. In addition to the discussions that took place in that seminar, I have benefited greatly from conversations with Kellie Robertson about the nature of pre- and early modern 'things' and from exchanges with Peggy Knapp, whose reading of the language of 'overspecification' in *Lear* has been immensely suggestive. The book would have never been written without the encouragement of the editors of the series, Ewan Fernie and Simon Palfrey, who have provided a welcome venue for a different kind of writing about Shakespeare. I here express my thanks to these individuals, with the understanding that none but me should be held responsible for any of the faults that may remain in the book they helped shape. Readers will find details about specific works referred to in the text in the 'Bibliographical Note and Further Reading' section, located at the end of this volume.

London, January 2008

Chapter 1

Shakespearean Metaphysics and the Drama of Immanence

Shakespearean what? The adjective Shakespearean gets applied to character flaws, moments of irony, certain types of tragedy or comedy. But metaphysics? What exactly does Shakespeare, a playwright known for his ability to 'hold a mirror up to nature', have to say about the organized study of ultimates: being, substance, unity and necessity? The premise of this book is that playwrights have as many things to say about these concepts as philosophers, but that they do so in their staging of theatrical reality, through the collective set of techniques that we refer to as dramaturgy. Shakespeare was just such a metaphysician, and we see him taking the measure of the world and its ultimate ordering principles when we examine closely the construction of three plays – *Twelfth Night*, *King Lear* and *The Tempest* – each of which illustrates what I will be calling Shakespeare's preference for a metaphysics of immanence over one of punctualism. In choosing the former, Shakespeare favoured a view of the world in which order and change are seen to emerge holistically from things themselves (immanence) rather than being localized in certain metaphysically isolated pockets of the universe (punctualism). We will be turning to three philosophers, Alfred North Whitehead, Henri Bergson and Baruch (Benedict) Spinoza in order to explore this contrast in depth and to say more precisely what a metaphysics of immanence is in each of these plays, but in consulting such an array of philosophers, we will not be hunting for their 'ideas' in Shakespeare's texts. For if it is true that Shakespeare valued immanence as a way of thinking about the very nature of being – locating the actor in the action, the player in play – then we should not expect him to 'voice' his metaphysics in a series of dramatic monologues. We are far more likely to find a distinctly Shakespearean metaphysics emerging from what the plays *do* and *are* rather than what they and their characters say. Indeed, the logic of Shakespeare's position is most obviously apparent in the phenomenal practice of the theatre: to appreciate it, we must look to the manner in which his plays take apart reality and then put it back together in a particular way, somewhat like an artist who builds a miniature ship, disassembles it and then raises it piece by piece within the confines of a bottle or glass.

The ship under glass in this case is not a physical thing, of course, but a series of actions and events held together by the theatrical rigging of entrances and exits, speeches, monologues and physically embodied actions. If the philosophers mentioned above can help us find the metaphysics in the motion of these plays, it will be because they too are vitally interested in characterizing a reality that is immanent or interpenetrating rather that boxed up in some special type of container – for example, a mind pinched off from the world or a body that interacts with only a discrete part of that world. Like the party of Italians who emerge from the sea in *The Tempest* only to marvel at the music that wafts across its shores, Whitehead, Bergson and Spinoza are fascinated by the ways in which truly distinctive forms of being fail to be bounded within the edges of a physical body, taking shape rather in an ensemble of actions, like the mobile shine of a school of fish turning in the water. Yet these thinkers are also interested in the reality and touch of the physical world in which we live, its pressing claims on our being and consciousness, something Shakespeare too never loses sight of in his theatrical practice. Finding our way to a truly Shakespearean metaphysics, then, should not be an exercise in transcendence, but an attempt to unearth a new and different kind of materialism, one that is grounded in bodies but emphatic in asserting the reality of their dynamic interrelations. A ship might very well be a hole in the water, but that doesn't mean the ocean is full of holes instead of ships: the abstract definition and the thing it defines are one and the same.

In this expansive spirit of inquiry, then, our task in these introductory pages will be to keep our attention focused on the theatrical situations in which Shakespeare's metaphysics emerges, and to recognize as well that there is something irreducibly abstract about the larger unity that these situations compose. The name we will be giving to Shakespeare's position as it emerges over the course of his career is 'dramaturgical monism', a position that we will find articulated most clearly in *The Tempest* and which we will approach through a discussion of Spinoza's substance monism. Dramaturgical monism and the theatrical practices associated with it must await full exposition in the final chapter of this book, but some of its key premises and corresponding theatrical techniques can be found in *Twelfth Night* and *King Lear*, which are treated in their own chapters with reference to the philosophies of Whitehead and Bergson respectively. Of course, these are different plays and different thinkers, and my aim in this book is not to say anachronistically that Shakespeare is a 'Whiteheadian', 'Bergsonian' or 'Spinozan'. Shakespeare is a Shakespearean, and while his metaphysics shares a common thread of interest with these philosophers, it could be explicated with the help of other writers in the metaphysical tradition as well. (Leibniz, Hegel and James come to mind.) There is something about the way these philosophers think the fluctuating and fundamentally indissociable nature of being, however – about their shared sense that metaphysical knowledge is a knowledge of our dynamic place in such a reality – that makes Whitehead, Bergson and Spinoza the nearly indispensable guides for thinking about a truly Shakespearean metaphysics as it emerges on stage. Because, as we will see, these philosophers refuse to model reality on spatially discrete bodies or materially indifferent ideas; they help us hear the metaphysical line that is part of the larger 'score' of *Twelfth Night*, *Lear* and *The Tempest*, calling our attention to the ways in which an immanent reality – one in which the whole of the thing is present in each and every part – unfolds in the real traffic on stage. Monism and an island reality that is both *of* the theatre and *of* the world: that is our destination, but to reach it we must return briefly to the question of what the word metaphysics might mean, for Shakespeare, and for us. This is not a simple task, since the meanings of the word metaphysics are as various as the writers who have used it.

* * *

When Shakespeare is actively writing in the sixteenth and seventeenth centuries, the word metaphysics is often used in connection with things magical or supernatural: it summons an entire kingdom of strange phenomena that, while out of the ordinary, can nevertheless be dreamt of in philosophy. Metaphysics, for example, is one of the topics recommended by Tranio to Lucentio as a topic for study in *The Taming of the Shrew* (1.1.37), one obviously more exciting than the study of 'virtue' that his master originally proposes for his time in Padua. Metaphysics is also the domain of Prospero's knowledge in *The Tempest*, a realm of arcane secrets that allows the old Duke of Milan to manipulate the weather and spirits of the island with super-human dexterity. Understood as a reservoir of hidden and therefore exotic knowledge, metaphysics begins to look like an avenue for masterful occult action, a mysterious means to unseen ends. But the word metaphysics is also used in Shakespeare's lifetime to refer to the organized study of being in and of itself: the attempt to say what is really real in the world and why it should be so. This tradition of metaphysical thought is drawn from ancient philosophers such as Aristotle, whose works and those of his commentators constituted the dominant intellectual strain throughout the Middle Ages and into Shakespeare's time. Writers working within this tradition tend to think of metaphysics as an inquiry into the first principles of things, a vocation that allows its practitioner to grasp the most basic and so durable aspects of the world in all of its changing qualities. According to this more classical definition of the term, metaphysics becomes the study of the different kinds of things that exist in the world, the nature of their interaction and being, and the principles that allow such basic entities to fit together into some larger whole.

Such an inquiry is by nature abstract, which is what allows metaphysics to posit connections between phenomena that look very different. Ask a sixteenth-century bachelor of arts to tell you the difference between an acorn, a human being and an angel, and he – university educations being for men in this period – will begin by telling you what these three things have in common. Each, he will point out, has something called a form that gives it definite properties and a capacity for change. But he will also try to say what makes these things stand apart. Acorns, for example, are made of matter and don't think; humans are made of matter and do; angels think without being made of any matter whatsoever. Our obliging scholar will have furnished us, in this instance, with a perfect example of how metaphysical explanations manage to extend their reach without crumbling under the sheer diversity of things in the world, a reach for which metaphysics will eventually be criticized in the twentieth century. In order to explain all that exists in some methodical way, the metaphysician works to provide basic distinctions that are assumed to apply to everything that exists – to everything that has being and so reality. In the case of the acorn, human and angel, the relevant distinctions are whether the thing is made up of matter, whether it has definite stable properties and whether it has the capacity to think or change. One could potentially organize the entire universe according to such scholastic distinctions, which is precisely what some of Shakespeare's contemporaries did when they chronicled the Great Chain of Being, an exhaustive hierarchy of things and creatures ranked from least to greatest, with stones and plants dwelling near the bottom, angels and God at the top.

But not everyone uses the same scheme or organizing intuitions to carve the world of 'what is' up into its component parts, which is what allows metaphysics to rise occasionally to the level of a Dante-like vision of the world or cosmos. Ancient philosophers of the Stoic,

Epicurean or Platonic sort had very different ideas about how to rank what was really real against what was merely apparent, and the average early modern individual could have widely varying interpretations of the underlying structure of the universe. (One sixteenth-century miller in Italy, for example, described the cosmos as being like a large piece of cheese from which emerged angelic worms, a vision that got him into considerable trouble with church authorities.) Arguably, it was the job of trained philosophers and theologians to keep the basic categories of existing things arranged in their proper places, making accommodations for observed facts, dogma or the 'revealed truths' of religion. As a playwright working in a theatre called 'The Globe', Shakespeare too would have been called upon to do this sort of metaphysical housekeeping of the universe, endowing objects, people and events with their own distinctive qualities and principles of change. Unlike his philosopher counterparts who did their work with syllogisms and concepts, however, Shakespeare did his metaphysical work with actors, sound, spaces and things. He used the specific resources of the theatre – that is, its physical limitations; its reliance on sound, speech and gesture; its indebtedness in performance to the passage of chronological time – to say equally specific things about the relatedness of beings in the world and their mutual participation in some larger, constantly changing whole.

It may have been somewhat easier for Shakespeare to think this way than other writers who produced fictional worlds in verse or written narratives because the theatre, as an embodied medium of performance, puts imagined life in a *real* bottle, subjecting it to a kind of automatic metaphysical analysis. For in telling a story with speaking bodies and relying on their phenomenal presence to produce theatrical effects, theatre must constantly cope with the immediate meaning of sensation and the limits of any one particular body's command of space. Indeed, theatre bears the explanatory burden of saying what is true of this actor, this situation, this moment, not just 'a time' that we happen once upon. Thus when the ghost appears on the ramparts in *Hamlet*, filling the watchmen's minds with 'thoughts beyond the reaches' of their 'souls', the play itself cannot help but generate questions about what it means to have a body and be in a particular place in space and time. How can a ghost – this ghost – tell the crucial tale of fratricide if it lacks a body that might produce sound? Does it, as the play later suggests of murder, speak with 'miraculous organ'? (2.2.571) How, moreover, does a king speak for himself and, simultaneously, with the collective voice of a kingdom? Is he given that voice by those who elect him? If so, how can a voice survive the death of the body that produces it, as is suggested in the final act of the play when Hamlet declares that Fortinbras 'has my dying voice'? (5.2.298) Does the actor speaking on stage have a similar, transitive vocal power? These are metaphysical questions – they call out for a broad definition or redefinition of some basic category (such as 'body') that underpins our grasp of the world – and a dramatist like Shakespeare seems particularly drawn to situations in which such questions are forced above board. As a dramatist, Shakespeare almost always takes the metaphysical bait, incorporating the categorical shivers or blurrings that are produced by situations on stage into rhetorical patterns that further attenuate the analysis that is being conducted on the level of immanent action. In *Hamlet*, this might mean producing a metaphysics of kingship in which the voice of the kingdom migrates from one body to another, evading the grasp of those who would treat it as a thing instead of a spectral inheritance. The point to remember here is that it is the *process* of acting out a story in a physical space that generates important questions and paradoxes, the very questions and paradoxes that spur a playwright and audience on to metaphysical themes – thoughts beyond the reaches of their souls. To say that the metaphysics of a Shakespeare play is immanent to its performance is thus to say that it emerges from the action in precisely this integral and organic way.

But if actions are the foundation of a theatrical metaphysics, we face special challenges in trying to examine them in performances that were conceived and executed over four hundred years ago. Some of the imaginative reconstruction implicit in such a project can be done by consulting stage directions, which are printed words describing the scenario and movements on stage, and by looking at documentary accounts of early modern staging practices. We can also consult the surviving words of the plays themselves, since they are an integral part of the way in which theatre advances its own action. (The survival of these words is, after all, what allows us to continue to perform the plays today.) In addition to recognizing that the words of the plays are like instructions for creating theatrical performances – diagrams of actions waiting to be performed – we might also remember that the very process of uttering words is a kind of action, which makes the hearing of those words another part of the theatrical event. How, then, ought we to understand the relationship between the words of these plays, which I will frequently be focusing on here, and the theatrical event that takes shape in and through them? If we think of theatre as a substance made up of embodied processes, what is it about the verbal as opposed to the gestural or physical aspects of those processes that gives them meaning within a larger metaphysical scheme?

Spoken language is crucial here because it is in words that Shakespeare often recognizes the fact that stage action is testing certain organizing principles that hold his theatrical universe together. The metaphysical line of a play thus emerges when basic concepts that make the action intelligible – concepts like time, being, will, cause, event, quantity, purpose, identity, body or environment – begin to attract attention as problems in and of themselves. Take, for example, the moment in Shakespeare's early play, *The Comedy of Errors*, in which one member of a pair of identical twins, Antipholus of Syracuse, describes his search for his long lost brother from whom he has been separated by shipwreck:

> *Ant. of Syr.* I to the world am like a drop of water
> That in the ocean seeks another drop,
> Who, falling there to find his fellow forth,
> Unseen, inquisitive, confounds himself.

So I, to find a mother and a brother,
In quest of them, unhappy, lose myself.
(1.2.35–40)

The Syracusan's language here is willfully paradoxical: the ongoing search for his cognate 'drop' in the ocean is described as beginning with a self who seeks, falls and then reflexively is confounded and lost, as if the seeker has become both the initiator and the victim of that ultimate loss. The more one thinks about Antipholus of Syracuse's quest to find the rest of his family, the more one senses a metaphysical question taking shape, metaphysical because it can't itself fully be answered with more action or experience. What makes one drop of water different from another, or even a thing distinct unto itself, if its edges are ultimately temporary? We don't have to delve into the grammar of symbolic logic to see that this speech deliberately puts the identity principle in doubt. For Antipholus of Syracuse and his long lost Ephesian brother, the weirdly algebraic sentences 'I am I' and 'I am not I' are both true. What then?

The rest of *The Comedy of Errors* will offer an answer to this question, using accidental meetings between various twins, their hair's-breadth near misses and oceanic depths of misunderstanding in order to suggest that memory and desire are what really individuate selves, not the physical features of bodies. The play does metaphysics, that is, by putting pressure on a seemingly basic concept like identity, showing where and how it might be incoherent, and then suggesting an alternative unity to the concept in the subsequent action that unfolds on stage. This procedure is different from the one envisaged by T. S. Eliot, who admired the 'metaphysical' practice of Renaissance poets like John Donne for their deliberate juxtaposition of dissimilar images in their poems. Unlike the aesthetic practice that Eliot describes, Shakespeare's deliberate movement through paradox and into action is not a device for creating shock or disjuncture, but the opening gesture of an emotionally engaged metaphysical analysis, one that unfolds with the aid of bodies on stage rather than propositions, lemmas or philosophical dialogue. Shakespeare may have been a myriad-minded writer, but his almost ridiculous ability to conserve radically different ideas in a single verbal pattern did not prevent him from thinking powerfully and explicitly about what unites the vast phenomena of the theatrical world on some deeper, holistic level. For Shakespeare, theatrical action became exciting precisely because it couldn't help but acquire a comprehensive metaphysical significance in the course of performance, one that might be shaped by the spoken word but that was its independent compliment as well.

This metaphysical tension between enacted events on stage and the spoken word is illustrated powerfully during the trial scene in *The Winter's Tale*, when the jealous tyrant Leontes brings his wife Hermione to a public trial for what he perceives to be her infidelity with his friend Polixenes. The exchange that takes place in act 3 begins with Hermione's challenge to the circumstantial evidence that has been arrayed against her. She does not know why the Bohemian king Polixenes has suddenly disappeared with the king's servant Camillo, an event that confirms Leontes's fears of being cuckolded, nor has she ever known the 'taste' of 'conspiracy' that their sudden departure has been made to suggest. To her declaration of innocence, Leontes responds:

> *Leont.* You knew of his departure, as you know
> What you have underta'en to do in's absence.

> *Herm.* Sir,
> You speak a language that I understand not.
> My life stands in the level of your dreams,
> Which I'll lay down.

> *Leont.* Your actions are my 'dreams'.
> You had a bastard by Polixenes,
> And I but dreamed it.

> (3.2.75–82)

Two interpretations are offered here concerning the relationship between imagined actions and real ones. Hermione says that Leontes is generating images of action (her conspiring with the Bohemian king after conceiving his bastard) that have no relationship to her own experience. The description of those actions, so conceived, cannot even be comprehended: they are another 'language'. Yet those conceptions are a weapon aimed at Hermione, which is why her life stands in the 'level' or path of flight of those fantasies that Leontes has aimed at her. Leontes, on the other hand, uses the language of predication to advance his interpretation of the fantasy–action relationship. Rather than being *like* what Leontes fears, Hermione's actions are those fears made real, so that the entire realm of fantasy has become level or continuous with that of action and events. The equation or ontological flattening effected by his proposition is obviously pathological, a product of the Sicilian king's paranoid jealousy. But the metaphysical principle behind the equation – that actions and ideas are fused and so interchangeable in some fundamental sense – articulates perfectly a principle that governs the larger arc of action in the play. While Leontes's jealous fits may indeed, as Paulina notes later in this act, be utterly childish and so merely imagined, the larger sweep of narrative action does indeed seem to *be* the sort of story that would be dreamt of by a child. It is for this reason that Shakespeare names his play after a goblin-story or 'tale' that's 'best for winter' in which the audience sees the child Mamillius whispering to his mother earlier in the play.

When we turn to *Twelfth Night*, *King Lear* and *The Tempest*, we encounter a different set of questions, no less abstract, and no less demanding of the attention of playwright and audience. Our task in the next few pages will be to briefly derive these questions from the plays and then to unfold their significance with the help of three philosophers whose zest for metaphysical inquiry is well known: Alfred North Whitehead, Henri Bergson and Baruch (Benedict) Spinoza. Although this trio of thinkers may seem historically and geographically diffuse – they are working in three centuries and as many countries – Whitehead, Bergson and Spinoza are really the ideal guides for a study of Shakespearean metaphysics. All three are immediately useful, as we will see, in clarifying the terms and significance of questions that are thrown up by the action and language of these plays, questions about the relationship of events to individuals, the interrelation of quantities and qualities and about the potential unity of experience in a single substance. The members of this group are also distinguished by their collective interest in the consequences of metaphysical thought and reflection – by their conviction that the fruits of such reflection must change our engagement with the *world itself* rather than simply 'clarifying' how the mind is able to understand it. As such, Whitehead, Bergson and Spinoza provide an alternative to the 'critical' philosophical tradition spawned by Immanuel Kant and his interpreters, a tradition that gives the mind rather than things in the world the determining role in shaping our experiences of the world. The appeal of this alternative tradition, of which Shakespeare is an important part, will be discussed in the final chapter of this book.

The main reason, however, for settling on Whitehead, Bergson and Spinoza as our tutelary spirits here is that, despite important divergences in their philosophical outlooks, they are united in their search for an immanent rather than transcendent order in events as they unfold in the world. It is this sense of immanence that I think best captures what is special about Shakespeare's metaphysics, a metaphysics which assumes that the being and quality of things is a function of their comprehension within other things and events, as if a universal power of touch has placed them all in proximity with one another without relying on the edge of a body to create zones of contact. Speaking more generally, we might characterize an immanent reality as one that lacks an 'outside' or numinous 'other place' that subtends or generates its immediate characteristics, just as it forbids local zones of 'transcendence' where the dynamics of worldly interaction are suspended or cancelled. Rather, an immanent reality is one in which the actual world always carries the burden of its own transformations, often through a dynamic process of change whose origins cannot be pinpointed in a single place or time. A metaphysics of immanence thus implies a certain skepticism about our ability to locate punctually all of the powers of an individual body or actor within that actor, as if they were a sort of metaphysical luggage that could be carried from one place to the next. Whitehead, Bergson and Spinoza were each skeptical of this edge-bound, encapsulated view of an agent's power in the world, and I will be arguing that what Shakespeare's plays presume to be true for their successful functioning *as drama* must itself stand as a challenge to the punctualist metaphysics that attracts the sustained criticism of these three thinkers.

I should mention at this point that the concept of immanence has been influentially discussed in connection with Whitehead, Bergson and Spinoza by the philosopher Gilles Deleuze, who used this concept to group these thinkers into a 'naturalist' or anti-transcendental tradition that he identified with his own philosophical concerns. Those familiar with Deleuze's work will recognize his influence in my choice of orienting philosophers here and may ask why I have not chosen Deleuze himself as one of the compass points in this study. Deleuze plays an important role in constituting a tradition of philosophers who are interested in immanence, but his own thought – as it develops in his work on cinema and in his later collaborations with Felix Guattari – ultimately takes the concept of immanence in a direction that is not naturally suited to the study of Shakespearean metaphysics. Particularly in the later collaborative work with Guattari, Deleuze's philosophy leads him to embrace a distinctly post-human conception of the body, a body that exists 'without organs' and so is dispersed into a world of intensity flows and their various 'territorializations'. As we will see in our discussion of these three plays, however, Shakespeare's metaphysics does not so much dissolve the human body as make it a co-production of the phenomena that come to define and maintain it: movement, voices, feelings, music and what Spinoza will call 'affection'. To remain true to the metaphysical line in Shakespeare's plays, then, we will be sticking with the three 'philosophers of immanence' who do not embrace this more dispersive account that becomes so fascinating to Deleuze. In doing so, we will be trying to understand how a particular kind of human being is preserved within – rather than scattered impersonally across – the emotionally charged worlds that Shakespeare creates, worlds that are ontologically capacious enough to make *all* phenomena part of a single being or thing, yet dynamic enough to make each of its phenomenal parts a distinct being of its own.

This Shakespearean dynamic of immanent definition and inclusion is acted out perfectly, for example, in the final recognition scene of Shakespeare's *Cymbeline*, a scene in which an astounding array of long-lost and mistaken characters are reunited with one another through a domino-like sequence of revelations. In this sequence, theatrical 'events' such as looking (and the acknowledgement of identity such an event implies) are dispersed into structures that defy what we might call the logic of punctualism, a legacy of Aristotelian and, later, Cartesian metaphysics that locates the properties of a particular worldly thing in the actual body that serves to individuate it and give it material existence. As King Cymbeline says of the wondrous exchange of glances in this spectacular staging of memories re-possessed, 'The counterchange / is severally in all' (5.6.397–98), which is to say, the glance of each person, reciprocally shared as it is with all others, is itself *in* all the others. Put another way, the sum of parts that make up the whole of this tessellated recognition structure is itself, as whole, present in *each* of its parts. Such a declaration is metaphysical because it reformulates the very notion of punctual being in a world where characters have become interchangeable (lover–rival; Briton–Roman); but it also has the effect of raising the action to a level of abstraction where the spatial disposition of that action can itself acquire a certain immanent significance. Crucial too is the fact that the structure described by Cymbeline suggests that the emotional effects of this final act of group comprehension has been multiplied: characters are not simply recognized by one another, but also affectively possessed by one another as the longing involved in unhoped-for recognition is folded into each point of the scene's geometry. This last point about emotional effect will be one we return to in readings of the individual plays, since some of the most profound affective turns in Shakespearean drama seem to come about when emotions are dispersed into the metaphysical fabric of the theatrical world.

* * *

The punctualism described above is both asserted and then undone in *Twelfth Night*, *King Lear* and *The Tempest*. For the remainder of this chapter we will briefly examine how each of these plays worries some aspect of the punctualist position and in doing so proposes an immanent metaphysics in its place. The key feature to grasp in this alternative vision Shakespeare offers in these plays is its unusual manner of configuring the relationship between material things – notoriously changeable and moveable according to the philosophical consensus of Shakespeare's time – and the forces that guide these things through the world. Such a distinction has been described with different terms in the past, each suggesting important metaphysical commitments: matter and form; body and soul; appearance and idea; object and number. The philosophical culture that Shakespeare grew up with was committed to the Aristotelian idea that an immaterial, unchangeable form was mixed with matter and that the combination produced something called a substance. In this so-called hylomorphic theory (where the Greek *hyle* refers to matter and *morphe* to form), a substance possessed both individuality and a logical or metaphysical unity, one that could be enumerated through comparisons with other substances. The philosophy to come, one that Shakespeare may have glimpsed in the Epicurus-inspired passages of Montaigne's *Essays*, was a mechanical one that turned its back on metaphysical forms inhering in things and instead identified individuals on the basis of their distinctive motions (or the motions of their parts). Descartes was one of the most successful advocates of the mechanical philosophy, dividing the realm of being into distinct kingdoms of thought and extension (the latter encompassing bodies in motion), allowing these two realms to interact only rarely, for example when a human being decided to move his or her body for a particular aim. In both the old and the new philosophies, the qualities or properties of a thing literally attached to the stuff of which it was made – stuff that served as the basis for all changes or alterations it would undergo. One reason why Shakespeare deserves to be placed in the company of Whitehead, Bergson and Spinoza, each of whom is a significant critic of Cartesian metaphysics and the punctualist worldview, is his refusal to make the being of a particular thing – whether we are talking about a thinking person, a perception, or a phenomenal attribute – a *property* of a single body and thus a purely local 'possession'. This does not mean, however, that Shakespeare and his anti-punctualist successors decided to 'lift the being of things' out of matter altogether and dissolve it into some kind of spiritualistic ether. He stuck to the reality of things, but thought that their identity was immanent to – or better, intertwined with – the situation or process in which they came to exist.

We will begin to take up these issues in Chapter 2 when we turn to Whitehead's philosophy of process and the drama of individuation or self-possession that defines the narrative arc of *Twelfth Night*. Possession is a significant term for theatre since it refers to the way in which an individual's identity gets taken up in some mental or bodily collection of stuff. To say that a particular someone, for example Antipholus of Syracuse, is 'lost' to himself is to suggest that his identity is something to be grasped or held on to like an object in space – a broken mast in a storm. It is just this metaphysical assumption of the spatial integrity of one's personhood or identity that gets muddled when a body seems to have been multiplied, which is the source of many of the misunderstandings in *Twelfth Night*, as it is for the earlier *Comedy of Errors*. But while the earlier farce seems to be a virtuoso juggling of bodies in space, *Twelfth Night* is much more a meditation on the power of 'occasion' – which in Renaissance parlance refers to a felicitous conjunction of circumstances or conditions – to produce or give birth to something that did not exist before: here

the hitherto confused twins, Viola and Sebastian, who find themselves face to face with one another in a dilated moment of mutual
recognition. Indeed, the language that is used to narrate and
comment upon that encounter in act 5 suggests that the meeting of
Sebastian and Viola is not so much a collision of pre-existing beings
(one twin punctually meeting the other in billiard-ball like fashion)
as an encounter or event that has managed to summon those two
beings into existence. The fact that occasion is given the power to
perform this creative act, if that is how we choose to interpret the
pivotal recognition scene near the end of the play, raises important
questions about the relationship between individuals and the processes of change they seem to undergo or emerge from. Having
acquired some sense of their proper being at the end of the play,
Sebastian and Viola are elevated to the status of what we might call
theatrical substances – self-standing unities with some comprehensive command of their own memories and feelings. If such a unity is
really a *product* of the penultimate scene rather than its condition, the
metaphysical question raised by the family reunion at the end of
Twelfth Night is this: what portion of their substance do Sebastian
and Viola owe to the events and occasions that brought them to this
final state? Is what we call a person or individual a collection of properties, a set of events in which he or she participates, or both?

This is just the kind of question that Alfred North Whitehead
grapples with in his 'philosophy of organism', a philosophy he proposes as an alternative to what he calls the seventeenth-century 'philosophy of mechanism'. According to Whitehead, the philosophy of
organism is a philosophy of process, one that provides a more rigor-
ous metaphysical underpinning for the study of nature and of human
thought taking place *in* nature than the one inherited from early
modern mechanists. With the rise of scientific rationality in the seventeenth century, Whitehead argues, European intellectuals such as
Galileo and Descartes inaugurated a powerful but nevertheless insuf-
ficiently abstract account of the nature of being, one that replaced the
Aristotelian ontology of substances discussed above. The difficulty

introduced by these thinkers, who simplified natural philosophy by limiting it to the study of matter in motion, was that they reduced every aspect of nature – all of its qualities, phenomenal diversity and changing appearances – to a collection of mechanical and, so, mathematically describable properties of bodies. But if extended bodies eventually came to replace Aristotelian substance as the foundational category of natural philosophy in the seventeenth century, the very notion of body and its attendant motions through 'simple locations' would likewise succumb, Whitehead argues, to new conceptual difficulties with the advent of quantum mechanics in the twentieth century. These developments cast in doubt the basic assumption that bodies of extended matter could, *pace* Descartes, 'possess' the property of motion or even be defined with reference to their motion alone. As an alternative, Whitehead tries to carve up the world of 'what is' in another way, in effect revising the metaphysical postulates of the seventeenth-century mechanists in order to make way for what he believes will be a broader, more comprehensive science. Events rather than extended bodies, he argues, ought to be seen as the most fundamental or primordial building block of all that is. Matter, bodies, the properties of things are thus, for Whitehead, not the foundation for the changes we observe in the world, but the product of those changes. Although the immediate inspiration for this move seems to come from developments in twentieth-century physics, Whitehead is really extending a line of thought that stretches back to Pythagoras, who believed that abstract entities like numbers could relate different parts of the world that seemed indifferently or self-sufficiently real. As with Pythagorean numbers, Whitehead suggests that there is something like a generalizeable contents of events or 'actual occasions' unfolding in the world, and that it is the abstract or metaphysical contents of occasions which allows *all* of the relationships among them to be generalized – to be given some character that is, to quote *Cymbeline* again, anchored and reflected 'severally in all'. To say that 'events are prior to things', which is one way of summarizing the thrust of Whitehead's metaphysics, is to say that occasions are in some sense the ultimate substance of experience: they are what all other things depend upon for their being and actuality, serving as the metaphysical base of relation (and so definition) for the phenomenal superstructure we are and inhabit.

Twelfth Night affirms this notion that occasion is the fundamental metaphysical building block of experience – certainly of experience in the theatre – and links the encompassing unity of occasion, which is to say, its role in relating part to dramaturgical whole and whole to dramaturgical part, to the immanence of theatrical personhood as it coalesces on stage. By being present to one another, Sebastian, Viola, and perhaps too Olivia and Orsino, are also *in* one another in the final recognition scene, suggesting the theatre's ability to create identities through mirrorings that play themselves out over theatrical space and through narrative time, but which ultimately take root in a metaphysical fabric or substance that is subject to its own rules. To take in hand the 'stuff' of theatrical illusion, 'such stuff as dreams are made on', and think about what *its* properties might be: this is the project of a playwright like Shakespeare who wants to see around the corner of theatre's ability to abstract bodies and spaces across the temporal arc of a story. One does not sense, for example, this straining against the notion of what Whitehead calls 'simple location' – being in a particular place at a particular time – in the dramaturgy of a master plotter like Shakespeare's contemporary, the playwright Ben Jonson, even if he is just as capable of thinking reflexively about what his theatre does as spectacle (his version of a moral mechanics). Jonson is committed to the unities of time and place, but he is also committed to the coherence of a space that pre-exists certain bodies and in a sense can entertain them with perfect indifference. One need think only for a moment about plays such as *Volpone* and *The Alchemist* to realize that Jonson's dramaturgy is resolutely punctual: it does not pinch or warp the shape of space and time, nor does it subordinate them *as categories* to some more fundamentally productive or organic reality. There are certainly times when one wonders if Jonson is not just behind the play, in the tiring room perhaps,

manipulating every detail of the performance no matter how spontaneous it may seem. But the particular vertigo one experiences in the
presence of Jonsonian staged play is ultimately the effect of a poetic
gambit, a cat and mouse game between concealed author and inquis-
itive audience. Shakespeare is playing a very different game when he
proposes that a single element in the theatrical spectacle – character,
event, action, body, music, feeling, scene – can become the vanishing
point or principle of generation for all the others.

Such theatrical experiments with metaphysical categories are not
limited to those involving bodies in space. We will find, when we
turn to *King Lear* in Chapter 3, that Shakespeare also puts into question the difference between quantity and quality, one of the most
basic distinctions we use to classify human knowledge – separating
the so-called natural from the human sciences – and a recurring
theme in the philosophy of Henri Bergson. Our reading of *Lear* will
focus on what one critic has called the play's 'odd running commerce
with quantity', a sensitivity to the significance of pieces and portions
that first makes its appearance during the disastrous opening love-
contest, where Lear's daughters are asked to measure out their affection for him in speech. 'What can you say', the king tells Cordelia in
the first scene of *The Tragedy of King Lear* (printed in the First Folio
of 1623), 'to draw / A third more opulent than your sisters?' (1.1.83–
84) Recalling the metaphysics of punctualism discussed above, we
find *Lear* restlessly interrogating the idea that feelings, familial roles
or even political identities can be mapped or spatialized, like a kingdom to be divided into its constituent parts. In its worst moments,
everything in *Lear* seems to have an edge or a bounding point, which
means that there is a point beyond which any given thing can no
longer be itself. Yet in saying that Lear's kingdom spans the lands of
France and Burgundy, or that his majesty encompasses the greatness
of 100 waiting men or so many words of praise, the characters in *Lear*
give 'local habitation and name' to something that defies any real
and discrete placement in the world of things. Indeed, the play provides some fairly grim answers to the bare metaphysical question of

how far a thing can be divided or augmented – love, a person, a kingdom – before it becomes something else, or nothing at all.

In a world where every quantitative reduction or copious rhetorical amplification seems to exhaust the thing described, leaving no fertile remainder, the very idea that quantity (men, land, praise) can somehow reliably express qualities (nobility, affection, remorse) becomes pathological. In Chapter 3 we will find that the play never gives an emotionally satisfying solution to this problem of division or exhaustion, where the self-conserving algebra of quantitative change becomes something like a tragic law. But *Lear* does suggest an alternative linkage between these two realms which does not locate qualitative feelings or experiences in an extended, edge-binding medium. This anti-Euclidian world, denied to Lear and his daughter in act 5, is one in which the qualitative realm is no longer mapped onto the quantitative, the relation being instead one in which *all changes in degree are changes in kind*. Quantities of love would thus not augment or decrease in such a world: as a quality, love would no longer have degrees, only varieties. On this reading, love names a collection of different feelings that are constantly in flux and so changing their very nature from moment to moment: such collection could not be reckoned by weighing it on a single scale. In contrast to the zero-sum logic of substance that infects Lear's conception of himself – one in which any division of a substance (kingship, majesty, paternity) leads to a corresponding diminution of that substance – we glimpse at the end of *Lear* an alternative, comic metaphysics in which time is boundlessly unfolding new kinds of beings and feelings rather than destroying static versions of 'older' ones. Here each moment would be a new species of time and feeling, a constantly ripening, immanent flux rather than a diminishing record of previous moments and passions.

This sensitivity to the metaphysics of quantity is not just apparent in the action and diction of *Lear*, but in the revisions that Shakespeare appears to have made to the play as it was adapted for the stage. Surveying some of these changes as they appear in the so-called 'First Folio' edition of *Lear*, the second half of this chapter follows out an idea offered by the critic John Jones, who noticed that revisions to the play cluster remarkably around various ways of expressing number and magnitude. (Significant differences exist between the first published edition of the play – a quarto edition that appeared in 1608 – and the one that appeared in the First Folio of Shakespeare's works published after his death in 1623. Folio and quarto are terms that refer to size of an early modern printed book, quarto being the smaller and generally less expensive of the two.) In the remainder of the chapter, we will see how Shakespeare's interest in such expressions such as 'seven stars', 'five wits' or 'two daughters' develops into an even fuller engagement with the qualitative resonances of various quantities when he decides to change certain numerical features of the text – for example, altering the first scene so that the word 'nothing' appears five times rather than three. Such an awareness of the complicated relationship between quantity and quality, manifest in the play's language, action and revision, leads us directly to the thought of Henri Bergson who claims that changes in the quantity of a sensation always result in a new and different *kind* of sensation *rather than an increase or decrease of the original one*, an insight he took from his critical engagement with the mechanical legacy of seventeenth-century thought. Like Shakespeare, Bergson knew that the tendency to think punctually about bodies, their limits and divisibility – aspects fungible through geometric or algebraic calculation – were ill suited for the analysis of feeling and experience, both of which unfold in a temporal flux. If the mechanical philosophy had the effect of spatializing time and so making it (and the changes it brings) thoroughly homogeneous, Bergson made time a generator of qualities and feelings so diverse that they could never march in place. Only by recognizing that every change in quantity is also a change in quality, he believed, would we be freed from the need to answer the obsessive and essentially empty question – Lear's question – of how far a thing can be divided before it ceases to be itself.

Bergson and Whitehead, we should notice, are both interested in how the intellectual scaffolding used to frame and raise the natural sciences in the seventeenth century brought with it certain assumptions about how the most basic building blocks of being – categories such as matter, body, motion, property, quality, event – are related to one another in a significant, comprehensive way. I have been suggesting that Shakespeare ought to be included in this conversation because he too, using the resources of the theatre, was able to explore precisely the relations among these metaphysical building blocks and to configure or re-configure them in suggestive ways. The plays are not proofs, nor are they arguments. But with the right kind of linguistic cues, positioning of bodies in space and arrangements of elements, Shakespeare's theatre can and does become a vivid staging ground for metaphysical propositions – events are prior to substance, every change in quantity is a change in quality – of the type I have been discussing above. We should go further, however, and say that much metaphysical writing tends to take place in an imaginary sort of theatre; that because metaphysics concerns the relationship of parts and wholes, it requires a sensorium in which such relationships can be dramatized. The specialized vocabulary found within certain philosophical texts ('numerical identity', 'substance', 'actual occasion', 'spatialization') should not distract us from this concrete need to enact and so comprehend a schematic vision, nor should it blind us to the propositional or diagrammatic value of events in drama that predicate certain kinds of things on other kinds of things. We have been thinking about Shakespeare as someone who uses language, action and events to posit such relations, to naturalize them or – and here we begin to use one of the most important words in metaphysics – make them seem somehow *necessary*. The theatre is uniquely positioned, as a spatial, embodied medium that unfolds its action over time, to support such metaphysical gambits. Not all playwrights or companies use it for this purpose, but Shakespeare certainly did, as we will see in the detailed readings in the chapters that follow.

But there is a further aspect of Shakespeare's dramaturgy that we need to introduce in order to set his plays within the larger tradition I have been describing here. When we say that a philosopher is committed to a metaphysics of immanence, we mean that he or she is unwilling to make the engine of being something that is either *completely outside* of the world or *completely encapsulated within some point of it*. The notion that divine interventions in human affairs are the actions of a removed manipulator whose essence is distinct from that of the world he or she acts on: this is the kind of global transcendence that an immanent metaphysics refuses. Such an interventionary scheme raises objections from philosophers for the same reasons that a *deus ex machina* is condemned by literary critics. There is something arbitrary about the idea that an immanent metaphysics distrusts. But there is also a local sort of transcendence that philosophers such as Whitehead, Bergson and – as we will see in a moment, Spinoza – have argued is equally unsatisfactory: the situation in which a physical cause or mind acts unilaterally on its immediate surroundings while remaining entirely indifferent to the complex of elements that make up the larger environment. This second, local form of transcendence can be thought of as a pinch in the metaphysical fabric of being, a region in which certain causal or mental acts have somehow been exempted – localized and partitioned away – from the complimentary activity of all those minds, perceptions and causes that make up the buzzing whole of the world. Bergson's response to this form of local transcendence is to deny the very notion that space and calculations of immediacy, length and continuity have any real bearing on phenomena such as feeling and memory, phenomena that are *just as real* as locally acting mechanical causes, but are not realized in the medium of quantified space. But there is another way around this problem, one that unties the punctual knot of space and time and, in doing so, dissolves their constraining power on causes, being and action. Instead of making parts of the totality independent of the whole – isolating them as mental or physical substances with the power to determine their immediate surroundings – one can argue that the distinction between the whole and its parts is itself illusory. What if the world is really just *one* entity in which every region is vitally alive with the power and force of every other region? What if individuals are not so much beings independent of one another as interwoven aspects of some larger being – modes or moments of a single substance that is more real than any of its isolated qualities? Under what conditions might we be able to think about and encounter such a substance in all of its interconnecting richness? In philosophy, we find it in the monistic metaphysics of Spinoza. In the theatre, it is Shakespeare's *Tempest*.

One substance, many modes: this is the founding principle of Spinoza's philosophy and the metaphysical intuition we will be invoking in Chapter 4 as we think about the fluid reality that is revealed in Shakespeare's *Tempest*. At the beginning of this Introduction, I said that Shakespeare was a dramaturgical monist, a term I used in order to suggest a parallel between Spinoza's commitment to a one-substance model of being and Shakespeare's tendency, most pronounced in the later plays like *The Tempest*, to view the elements of theatrical reality as interconnected features of a single whole – aspects of what we might call the substance of theatrical reality. As the root of the term suggests ('mono' meaning single or one), monism is an interpretation of being that takes its inspiration from the thought of oneness. For those who are new to his philosophy, the greatest difficulty posed by Spinoza's monism is the sheer number of consequences that follow from this single innovation, consequences we will be exploring in our reading of the play throughout this final chapter. Substance, we should remember, is an Aristotelian term for anything that stands on its own – anything that possesses its own metaphysical integrity and so supports the changing phenomenal features that can be said to belong to it. If he were real, *Lear*'s Gloucester would be a substance in the Aristotelian sense: his loss of sight belongs to him, not the other way around. In the seventeenth century, both Aristotelians and Cartesians advocated metaphysical schemes in which substances were thought of as plural: for orthodox Aristotelians, there was the Great Chain of Being that ordered an array of different *kinds* of substance (plants, worms, humans, angels) into a hierarchy of increasing metaphysical perfection. For Cartesian dualists, who opposed this varietal model, the number of kinds of substance in the world could be reduced to two: substances that thought (God, angels, human souls) and those that were extended (bodies). Although there was disagreement within and across these groups as to how substance might be understood or cognized, both the original Aristotelian substance model and the Cartesian dualist one posited multiple substances (of however many varieties) moving about the world in relative independence. Different aspects of our phenomenal experience of the world could thus be understood by locating the causes of any observed change in one substance or another, substance now being understood as a container or staging point for action and natural effects.

In saying that there is one substance rather than many, Spinoza complicates the relationship between the local sources of action (whether they are conscious beings or simply moving objects) and the points where that action is made manifest to sense. A relationship *does* exist between metaphysical actor and outcome, as we will see, but that relationship can be grasped only in the context of the total environment of thoughts and bodies, thought and body being the two attributes under which the human mind can comprehend this single substance. One would expect that such a unifying move would have a homogenizing effect on our experience of the world, collapsing body into body, ship into storm, until all that remains is a humming blob. But when Spinozan unity is understood as metaphysical rather than phenomenal – when we see that things are one in *substance* rather than phenomenal appearance or physical location – something very different happens. The great diversity of particular things and events in the world is actually preserved rather than diluted: such diversity comes to be seen as vitally dependent, in fact, on a metaphysical foundation that can guarantee that diversity in all of its forms. The key point to remember here is that the relation of parts to whole is immanent, which means that neither is disposable in the analysis of what is really real. Thinking monistically in a Spinozan vein, then, turns out to be a novel strategy for intensifying one's appreciation for the discrete phenomenal elements in a world, one that heightens *their* unique being by making them part of *a* unique being. This intensification can occur in the theatre, where the world is taken apart and then reassembled in a focused theatrical space, or it can occur through reflection on the nature of substance, which is the programme of Spinoza's major work, *The Ethics*.

What leads Spinoza to adopt this position? Like Shakespeare, he is fascinated by the problem of how individual beings are related both to one another and to some larger whole – a problem that becomes particularly vexing for Spinoza when he confronts Descartes' division of the world into the two substances of mind and extension. How, Spinoza begins to wonder, can a mind ever interact with some region of extended substance when the two share absolutely no common feature? Can mind physically move matter, even though it lacks a body of its own? Can a portion of the phenomenal, embodied world ever find a means refined enough to tickle a bodiless substance like mind? Leaving behind Descartes' substance dualism, Spinoza argues that the realms of thought and extended matter are each attributes of a single substance famously called 'God, or Nature', one that expresses itself in the two attributes that Descartes had treated separately. Humans are, and this is a crucial feature of the scheme, part of this single substance, which means that we are *one of many aspects* of an integrated, self-altering whole. But as soon as we accept the monistic view of being, questions of action and existence – the kinds of questions that so trouble Hamlet in his private moments – must be rethought from the ground up. What would it mean for one part or region of this substance to 'act' on another? Isn't this really the same thing as a being acting upon itself, in which case 'acting' is really a strange word? Why not just say that the being changes? We get a sense of just how radical Spinoza's solution to the problem of substance dualism is when we start asking these questions with the new monistic assumption in place.

To say that Shakespeare was inclined to dramaturgical monism is to say that he was sympathetic to the monist's vision of how all things are connected, and was perhaps driven towards it as he thought reflexively about the nature of action in the theatre. We have already begun to glimpse how characters and events in *Twelfth Night* and *King Lear* become participants in events or structures that cannot be apportioned to particular points of time and space, and so how these plays use a mixture of action and words to redefine the basic building blocks of reality in the theatrically represented world. The dramaturgy of these plays suggests an artist deeply aware of the ways in which the substance of theatrical reality itself – its physical translations of being, events, and actions – is available for questioning and even reconfiguration, which is how theatre becomes a medium for metaphysical experimentation. In *The Tempest*, Shakespeare's career-long interest in the limits of the punctualist worldview expresses itself in an explicitly monistic or 'island' metaphysics, one in which each part of the theatrical world can act on any another (regardless of 'distance') by virtue of their mutual immanence and interpenetration. While there are certainly monistic intuitions in the earlier plays – the realm of quality or 'intensity' in *Lear*, for example, is impossible to parse out into subdivisions or primitive metaphysical units – these intuitions are not generalized into a global metaphysical vision in quite the comprehensive way that they are in *The Tempest*. It may be an accident of history that Shakespeare arrived at this vision late in his career, but I suspect that, given his earlier interest of the nature of process and flux in the theatre, Prospero's island must have struck Shakespeare as an extraordinarily powerful embodiment of the immanent reality he experienced on stage as both dramatist and audience member. Metaphysically speaking, this 'island of one' is certainly the most elegant response to the question of how the parts of an evolving theatrical reality are related to one another and, in the process, to some larger whole. It is on the basis of its comprehensive integration of metaphysical vision with dramaturgical practice, then, that I choose *The Tempest* as the exemplar of Shakespeare's metaphysical position, although that position may have been more of an inclination with varying expressions.

As with *Lear*, *The Tempest* offers a critique of the punctualist conception of action by contrasting it with an alternative, in this case, ambient mode of action and interrelation among things. Prospero is a living embodiment of what we might call the locally transcendent actor, a magus whose apparent indifference to the forces around him allows him to shape and change his environment in a focused, punctual way. Like one of Jonson's plotters, Prospero *himself* is tied to the landscape through his physical being, something he and the audience remember when the great orchestrator must interrupt the wedding masque in order to deal with the plot against his life. Yet the instruments of Prospero's self-possessed brand of action are specifically exempt from the logic of place that constrains the hand of their master. Ariel, for example, brags of an almost elemental fluidity of being when he tells Prospero of his exploits in act 1:

> I boarded the King's ship. Now on the beak,
> Now in the waste, the deck, in every cabin
> I flamed amazement. Sometime I'd divide
> And burn in many places; on the top-mast,
> The yards and bowsprit would I flame distinctly;
> Then meet and join.
>
> (1.2.197–202)

What kind of substance is Ariel? The language here, recalling as it does the phenomenon of St Elmo's Fire, is chosen to suggest a body that is divisible *across* places. The actor playing Ariel, of course, is a living breathing person, an epicene youth who can perhaps be hoisted aloft on stage. But when the actions of this putatively ubiquitous self-divider are attended by a similarly fluid theatrical music, the dramaturgical combination becomes a revelation of sorts. The substance of this place – be it an island, a theatre or some basic quantum of imaginary space – ought to be thought on the model of music, and it is in the subtle orchestration of music and bodies that Shakespeare finds the model for a single theatrical substance with many modes.

The action of *The Tempest*, then, becomes a progressive exposition of the ambient quality of theatrical reality, its presence to itself in some tactile but nevertheless diffuse way. Prospero is, in a sense, the one who must be educated in the ways of this superordinate substance, even though he seems to be the master of its local manipulations. That exposition occurs through the staging of action, ranging in mood from the farcical interactions of Stephano and Trinculo with Caliban to the ethereal ministrations of Ariel as he draws Ferdinand to Miranda by means of a song. What we find in these contrasting scenes of movement and action is that the relationships between bodies on stage and the environment they occupy is constantly being subjected to scrutiny; with every subtle change in an agent's power over (and so, separation from) a given portion of his or her environment, there is a corresponding change in the mood that pervades the scene. Indeed, after enough comparisons of this sort, we find that certain kinds of music-action combinations represent distinctive emotional dispositions, not just of the characters or the audience, but of the theatrical world itself. As the metaphysical analysis of bodies and music opens onto questions of mood and emotion, we discover something surprising in *The Tempest*. The play is not a neo-Platonic allegory about the power of music to enable action on a cosmic scale. It is, quite the contrary, an extended tutorial – by means of action and music – in the ethical and emotional consequences of our immanent immersion in the world, one that suggests that punctual action on such a world is often both tyrannical and illusory. Shakespeare thus tries to do with *The Tempest* something that Spinoza tries to do with *The Ethics*, albeit with different means: to illustrate the virtues of immersion in a body and all of its diverse powers and to show how openness to affection – which is an openness to the interconnected climate system of moods and emotions that one substance implies – is a satisfying way of engaging with the world.

In a sense, the process envisioned here is something akin to bobbing in a turbulent sea: it implies a kind of salutary coping that is practised involuntarily, but which nevertheless involves an invigorating immersion in the medium in which one lives and moves. We might recall, in this connection, the image of Sebastian that appears at the beginning of *Twelfth Night*, when the Captain describes his last glimpses of Sebastian in the wreck to his sister:

> *Cap.* I saw your brother,
> Most provident in peril, bind himself –
> Courage and hope both teaching him the practice –
> To a strong mast that lived upon the sea,
> Where, like Arion on the dolphin's back,
> I saw him hold acquaintance with the waves
> So long as I could see.
>
> (1.2.10–16)

We may not want to identify with the peril of this situation, but the 'acquaintance with the waves' described here is precisely the kind of engaged play and high-stakes immersion that seems appropriate to the reality Shakespeare will articulate many years later in *The Tempest*. Courage and hope become the teachers; music draws the singer across the waves. Let us test the waters in earnest now, as we turn our attention to *Twelfth Night* and the coping powers of Sebastian's twin.

Chapter 2

Whitehead and the Final Satisfaction of *Twelfth Night*

Letters and documents are sometimes stamped 'time sensitive', but the label might just as well be used to describe events, particularly events coming to pass in the theatre. Nowhere is this more true than in *Twelfth Night*, a play that unfolds like an exotic perennial as it moves towards its final climactic scene, the reunion of the separated twins Viola and Sebastian. The emotional richness of their reunion derives from the intensity of what we might call its spatio-temporal implication in the rest of the play's action – the way in which this particular family reunion knits together all the strands of plot development and stage antics that have precipitated it. Even audiences who have seen the play before tend to get caught up in the swelling crest of action that seems finally to break in the final scene. How is it that Shakespeare has managed to pivot so many emotions – longing, grief, reconciliation, relief, joy – on a misunderstanding, on the accidental reunion of twins separated by shipwreck? The dramatic effect that is produced when 'one face, one voice, one habit' is divided into 'two persons' is itself quite calculated, of course, the result of a long string of mishaps and plot strands that have been gathered together in a single bundle of dramatic energy. The spontaneous quality of this final recognition has long struck critics as buoyant, sweet, masterful, all qualities that develop out of the complicated dependence of the final event on the chance meetings, misrecognitions and wayward schemes that have brought the twins, their lovers and their antagonists together in Olivia's garden. Indeed, words like fortune, accident and 'occasion' – the latter referring to a bald Renaissance goddess whose solitary forelock was said to represent fleeting opportunity – occur at crucial moments throughout the play, alerting audiences to the work of some kind of creative deity or third hand working the scenes and movements of the play.

Shakespeare's original audience would have recognized the link between the frequent allusions to fortune and 'cohering circumstances' and their own culture's highly qualitative sense of time. One finds regular references in writers such as Francis Bacon to the 'quality of the times' in a given monarch's reign, a formulation that suggests that time itself is a container with certain overriding qualities. Renaissance audiences were also familiar with ideas popularized by Machiavelli and others who praised the virtues of the fox, arguing that effective action often requires an exquisite sense of timing, of judging exactly when to reveal something, when to take a risk or when to remain silent. These associations call attention to the complexity and contingency of the falling-together-of-circumstances in the conclusion, circumstances that carry with them a certain emotional colouring because of their conditional nature. The action seems to carry itself along with a kind of immanent, self-determining force, as if a troupe of marionettes has cut its own strings and now stands, blinking, at the threshold of life. Viola, who with her brother is trading lines of what seems like a single speech – it is really the recitation of their shared history – is the most eloquent in describing how circumstances have in effect donated to the characters a second chance at happiness. She declares to Sebastian:

> *Viol.* If nothing lets to make us happy both
> But this my masculine usurped attire,
> Do not embrace me till each circumstance
> Of place, time, fortune do cohere and jump
> That I am Viola, which to confirm
> I'll bring you to a captain in this town
> Where lie my maiden weeds, by whose gentle help

> I was preserved to serve this noble count.
> All the occurrence of my fortune since
> Hath been between this lady and this lord.
>
> (5.1.242–51)

In one sense, the reunion foreshadowed by the initial shipwreck and separation of twins has become a dramaturgical fact: it is physically embodied in the arrangement of the twins' bodies on stage and verbally manifested in the announcement – here, the first time in the play – of Viola's name. In another sense, however, that reunion is virtual, sitting somewhere on a horizon that the play is positing but cannot yet reach. Viola is telling Sebastian that they must *wait* to embrace each other as brother and sister until she obtains her 'woman's weeds' or clothes from the sea captain. The real reunion, if we take her words at face value here, requires that certain elaborate conditions – understood spatially as a set of ill-sorted objects – must 'jump' one with another like the joints of a well-made doll or piece of furniture. Indeed, the peculiar grammar of the passage allows Viola to speak the scene's strange conditional truth as if it were a present fact: do not embrace me until these circumstances cohere and jump . . . have they? . . . that I *am* Viola. Metaphysically speaking, the crucial point here is that it is the gathering of place, time and fortune that will enable Viola finally to become herself in this play, even as the causal relationship between such an abstract process of coherence and her 'becoming Viola' remains unclear.

These are rich and complicated lines, some of the most dramatically powerful that Shakespeare wrote. They acquire this complexity because the thoughts that are spoken here are as much a part of the event as the physical meeting of twins, the fact of the crowd on stage, and the physical geometry of their placement. All the theatrical elements cohere, jump together, like charmed or attracted particles. But if the scene refers us to some future moment in which the recipe for Viola's identity – the process that is about to give her an 'I am' – will be fulfilled, it also points us backward, to a series of moments in which characters commit themselves to waiting for occasion to bring about the right circumstances for action. Viola especially, but also Olivia and Maria, seem quite aware of the fact that their plans are what we might call 'eventual' – that they must hitch the wagon of their desires to the changing flux of circumstance if there is to be any satisfaction. In the Renaissance ideology of self-assertiveness, such a cultivation of chance was usually the prerogative of forward-looking males: only the bold man, the aristocratic lore went, could discipline the goddesses of Fortune or Occasion and bring them to heel. The situation in *Twelfth Night* is somewhat different, since it is often women who have the power to discern auspicious moments for action. As we will see, this is both a matter of discipline and trust, but it implies knowledge of the fact that certain kinds of events – creative, singular events that could not be foreseen by any one person – are positively indebted to the twin powers of fortune and occasion to bring them about. The more unique and unprecedented the outcome, the more complicated and unforeseeable its causes have to be. (In early modern English, the word 'event' literally meant 'unforeseen outcome', a meaning that the word began to lose as statistics became the chosen language for discussing contingency.)

But Viola's declaration to Sebastian suggests an even deeper debt to fortune, occasion and the powers of circumstance, one that is assessed in the realm of identity and individuality. Time-sensitive events that depend on landscapes, bodies and memories being just so are not simply curiosities – the kinds of things that make an onlooker like Olivia exclaim 'Most wonderful!' (5.1.219) They are part of the *process* whereby individuals, those time-honoured substances of classical metaphysics, become themselves. Viola and Sebastian do not arrive on the scene and find one another standing there, like billiard balls that have finally managed to collide. As the words of the play suggest, these two are actually one, and what the scene promises is separation, distinction and ultimately, individuation. When the process that is initiated here reaches its full conclusion – off stage, perhaps, or in some final dance? – we will have the promised comic satisfaction, and these speaking substances that Viola refers to as ghosts or 'spirits' will be seamlessly clothed in flesh and blood. This final occasion must be creative, a form of birth, in that it will precipitate a daughter from what was once a hypothetical pair of twins-in-one: 'I am all the daughters of my father's house', Viola opines hopelessly earlier in the play, 'And all the brothers too' (2.4.119–20). Such a birth is a restoration of an identity that, paradoxically, can never punctually exist so long as it is in-the-making: the future is always 'in' the past, but the past is always making anticipatory detours through a future yet to come. Viola herself *is* this anticipatory progress and flux, not a thing 'prior' – awaited by 'her', a 'brother', or an audience member sitting like 'patience on a monument' – nor a 'substance' that 'was' in the play virtually and then finally arrived in actuality. She will only be named at the end, and even then, in an oddly anticipatory fashion. The play keeps its most novel entity, Viola herself, dispersed over time and dependent on its flux even in its final lines with their conditional 'if': that's what it means for process to generate a substance instead of the other way around.

I have described this scene in deliberately Whiteheadean terms, although this may not be obvious to those who have never read the philosopher's works. Veteran readers of *Science and the Modern World* or *Process and Reality*, two texts in which Whitehead elaborates his 'process metaphysics', may have already heard echoes of his thinking in the language of occasion, satisfaction, coherence and event. One does not have to work hard, in fact, to re-describe the theatrical transactions of *Twelfth Night* in Whiteheadean terms. The theatre speaks the language of events and process, which for Whitehead are the basic building blocks of reality. Indeed, what the final reunion in *Twelfth Night* shows us, in fact, is that all theatre is built out of what Whitehead calls 'actual occasions': minimal or atomic units of reality in which the utter multiplicity of the universe is bundled into synthetic moments of 'satisfaction', a process that is variously described in terms of feeling, perception and a type of appetitive grasping called 'prehension'. These are all technical terms in Whitehead's philosophy, and I will attempt to offer analogies to explain them in the course of my exposition of events in the play. The important thing to keep in mind when approaching Whitehead's metaphysics for the first time is that he is trying to do two things which we have already begun to think about in previous sections. First, he is attempting to reformulate the 'substance' metaphysics of his predecessors in a way that makes the process of change *more fundamental* to an account of reality than any punctual or spatialized description of the discrete 'substances' in which change is manifest. (He is trying to put the ocean in the bottle instead of the ship.) Second, he is looking for a vocabulary that will help him think through and explain the radical immanence of each piece of reality to all others and to the whole that they represent. As someone who has thought a great deal about the logic of mathematical sets, Whitehead is particularly attracted to concepts that allow him to think about membership, participation, inclusion and relation between different elements in his intellectual scheme. One could think here of a children's 'find a word' puzzle in which portions of a grid of letters are circled and thus organized into words, with some letters 'participating' in more than one word. If we were to imagine twisting and folding that grid in such a way that a potentially limitless number of words and intersecting circles were generated from moment to moment, we would be thinking about reality in a typically Whiteheadean way.

When discussing individuals, then – which for Whitehead are entities whose character or identity *is* their process of change and becoming – he adopts a vocabulary that transforms reality into a series of gatherings, somewhat like the 'gatherings' of printed pages that book binders collect and then sew into a 'quire'. If we think of these gatherings not as physical pages but as metaphysical events – moments in which a new page has been folded into reality – we begin to see how Whitehead's vision of the universe implies a certain creativity at the heart of being, one whose signature or trademark is the singular novelty of each new occasion that includes, and in doing so transforms, all the others that surround it in space and time. As Whitehead will say in

Process and Reality, 'the many become one, and are increased by one' (21), a remark that suggests the gathering of entities which he terms an 'actual occasion' *is itself an entity*, and so contributes to the singularity of each occasion as it comes into concrescence. But this novelty does not preclude what he will at times refer to as the 'solidarity' of each occasion with every another. Elsewhere in a text entitled *Modes of Thought,* he will write, 'The world is included within the occasion in once sense, and the occasion is included in the world in another' (224). Whitehead's use of the logical term 'inclusion' here is deliberately abstract: it goes beyond any spatial sense of 'containing' that one might associate with it. Yet it is just this additional abstract force that makes it useful for thinking about the dramaturgical and emotional effect that Shakespeare is trying to achieve at the end of *Twelfth Night.* For what is the value of Viola's stepwise, oblique approach to the union of memories promised in the last scene if not the radical gathering up or inclusion of past occasions witnessed in the play into yet another event that is both inevitable and unexpected, immanent but transcendent? While I think Whitehead's ideas would be useful for thinking about all kinds of events in the theatre, his view of the priority of process is suggestive for thinking about this play in particular because *Twelfth Night* is so insistent in foregrounding the creative power of occasion and its foundational role in securing individual identities. We shouldn't feel compelled, then, to read Shakespeare's play as an extended example of Whitehead's theories. Far better to treat *Twelfth Night* as a metaphysical statement on its own, one whose priorities and assertions of value are really only brought into clearer focus through comparison with Whitehead's ideas.

To understand Shakespeare's analysis of the priority of events over substances, we will be focusing primarily on the quality of this final occasion and the theatrical transactions that bring it about, asking how it was built and what metaphysical principles this construction might express. The result will be an increased appreciation for Shakespeare's own theatrical assertion that the nature of identity is not that of an object but of an event and – picking up another

Whiteheadean theme – his sense of the creativity of occasion, that third hand which continuously cuts the deck as time uncovers the cards, one by one.

* * *

A play or a performance is an event. So too, the climax of a drama or its conclusion, inasmuch as both can be referred to with their own words, are also events. These events can have qualities, as Aristotle once pointed out, being terrible, happy, devastating, necessary, awful, avoidable or trivial. But what do we mean when we say that the play is designed to bring a certain *kind* of event about, and that this kind of event is an expression of the temporal process in which it unfolds? What exactly does 'time sensitive' mean when we are talking about events, and is there more than one way to interpret this phrase? How, moreover, can we talk about events in the world of the theatre without asking what it is about the theatre that makes events – changes of fortune that come about by action, inertia, accident or circumstance – so important? Some further definitions are necessary.

When we say that something has 'happened', what we usually mean is that a change has occurred in a particular state of affairs and that the *activity* or event of that change is separable – conceptually, at least – from some situation that was first one way, then another. You are in the theatre. You think to yourself, 'something is happening!' The thought is a common one, perhaps so common that you are not fully able to grasp its importance in the course of your experience in the theatre. Yet events and the fact of their occurrence are the most basic units of any theatrical experience, the minimal foundation which any such experience presumes as a condition of possibility, even if the 'happening' in question is the absence of any sensible action. (One thinks here of the tension that develops in Samuel Beckett's *Breath*, a drama with no characters that lasts for approximately 25 seconds.) Because theatre is a temporal medium – because, unlike a painting, it moves – it is constantly building meaning into the open possibility of change. Acknowledging that possibility as a fact of the performing situation is a key aspect of the theatrical experience, both for the actor and the audience. For in saying to him or herself 'now, perhaps, or a little later, the present will no longer resemble the past', the theatre-dweller is agreeing that a certain kind of time – time as a yardstick for change or movement – is real, as real as anything else in the theatre. And if time is real, then events or changes of affairs are always there to be witnessed or waited for, audiences scanning the action of a given plot for a point where some sort of outcome or result has become inevitable. If the letter from Friar Lawrence had only arrived on time, the audience of *Romeo and Juliet* thinks, then the final deaths of the two lovers might have been avoided. The conclusion of Shakespeare's tragedy is doubly time sensitive, first because it depends on a message that ceased to do its job the moment it was late, and second because it gathers up the characters and feelings that have been building throughout the play and twists them, in the final act, into something entirely and awfully new. When we decide to call Juliet's suicide a pivotal event – it is certainly the rawest moment in the play – then we agree that certain changes of affairs in the theatre take their flavour and perhaps their very existence from their dependence on, and interpenetration with, other events. Like time itself, action on stage is *always* inclusive: it can't help but encompass what goes before it and what will follow.

Twelfth Night is no tragedy, of course. Its paths converge in a garden rather than on a funeral pyre. Where and how the careers of various characters (and thus their stories) meet goes a long way towards defining how a play like *Twelfth Night* satisfies comic expectations. There is a geometry to this kind of comedy, just as there is a geometry to tragedy. But that geometry is not static, like a two-dimensional figure on a chalkboard. Indeed, in the case of *Twelfth Night,* we have before us a moving diagram that charts how a troupe of theatrical 'substances' manages to acquire a kind of immanent identity through their changing, novel reconfigurations with one another. In a non-trivial way, this is the story about how what happens makes you what you are. As we will see in a moment, that diagram is traced physically by bodies moving about the stage, but it is also traced *metaphysically* in the abstract coherence of what Shakespeare calls 'place, time and fortune'. Such a metaphysical coherence is, for Shakespeare, the organic and emotional unity of the theatrical occasion – a singularity that actors and audiences participate in but that they cannot literally possess as they would a ring or a purse. The process unfolds through the usual dramatic means: characters arrive on stage and obstacles are encountered; designs are hatched and enabling misunderstandings are introduced without being fully cleared up; characters arrive by chance or design at moments that either advance the schemes that are being hatched on stage or launch them in a new direction. One can imagine the stage in this play as a movable window in the hedge of a Renaissance knot garden, one of those maze-like structures that is constantly re-partitioning space into containers that conjoin other spaces or dwindle into dead ends. As they make their way through that maze, Viola and Sebastian are engaged in a constant process of hiding and unveiling, giving out pieces of themselves in environments where their real identity cannot be entirely grasped. The key to Shakespeare's dramaturgical strategy in *Twelfth Night* is to keep both elements in the drama – the garden 'rooms' and the people who occupy them – in motion, so that actions are launched in one place but their careers are effectively altered as a new environment takes shape around them.

Consider, for example, the crucial moment in the fifth act when Olivia, who has just been espoused to the man she thinks is Cesario (but is actually Sebastian), arrives on stage in the wrong room of the garden, taking Viola for her newly minted husband. After asking 'Cesario' several times why he is not responding to her requests, Orsino erupts in a rage, deciding to leave and taking his servant with him (where, exactly?) to spite the unreceptive Countess. Viola is only too happy to go with the man she secretly adores, declaring that she loves her master more than she will 'ever love a wife'. The matter comes to a head, now, as the meaning of the words spoken by two of the bodies on stage (Olivia and Viola) are effectively 'displaced':

> *Oliv.* Ay me detested, how am I beguiled!
> *Vio.* Who does beguile you? Who does do you wrong?
> *Oliv.* Hast thou forgot thyself? Is it so long?
>
> (5.1.135–37)

Who indeed? The question is unanswerable at this point, not because Viola is unwilling to play along, but because circumstances have not yet conspired to make clear exactly what Viola *is* at this moment. Servant or noblewoman? Man or woman? 'Who does beguile you?' is exactly the right question to put to this dramaturgical situation as a whole, not just to Olivia in her impatience.

The moment harks back to an earlier one in which Viola, newly arrived on the shores of Illyria, is discussing possible courses of action with the sea captain who has dragged her from the waves. The captain tries to console Viola's grief for the loss of her brother with an analogy: you were saved by chance, so perhaps your brother was saved too. Viola is open to the captain's suggestion – 'mine own escape unfoldeth to my hope, / Whereto thy speech [about my brother's survival] serves for authority' (1.2.17–18) she says – and with increasing vehemence declares her allegiance to chance, 'hap' (happenstance) and the inscrutable fluctuations of 'occasion'. (The Latin root of 'occasion', *casus*, is the word for chance.) This allegiance is signalled in two ways, first through the mention of terms explicitly associated with chance and contingency, but secondly through the syntactical and grammatical choices she makes in describing her hopes for the future. That future is dominated by process – the flux of events which can be accommodated but not commanded – and so the changes on the horizon are expressed in the passive voice. When told about the misfortunes of Countess Olivia, herself deprived of both a father and a brother in the course of a year, Viola declares:

> *Viol.* O that I served that lady,
> And might not be delivered to the world
> Till I had made mine own occasion mellow,
> What my estate is.

> (1.2.37–40)

The notion that certain times or 'occasions' can be ripe (mellow) for action – in this case, the revelation of her social station – is an obvious nod to the Renaissance doctrine of the quality of times. It is also a reference to the ancient Greek concept of *kairos*, which designates a kind of rare but 'opportune moment' which the masterful actor and speaker can recognize and then exploit for his or her own ends. Here, just as in the speech quoted from the concluding reunion scene in the previous section, Viola is declaring that something is *not* going to happen until the occasion is just so. The metaphysical outlook here is one that assumes the world or environment is always 'doing' something and that the individual's plan of action – even crucial aspects of her identity – are themselves conditioned by that action. Viola is not hopeful for her brother's survival because *she escaped*; her escape 'unfolds' to her 'hope' the same wish that she has for her brother (whom 'courage' and 'hope' taught to 'hold acquaintance with the waves'). She will not reveal her true identity in Illyria, but that identity will 'be delivered to the world' once she has 'made' occasion ripen or mellow. We ought to appreciate the paradox involved in imagining that Viola is simultaneously going to *make* something happen, and that that something is really an activity which she has no direct control over (the ripening of occasion).

If this sounds painfully indirect, it's supposed to be. Shakespeare is interested in putting this character on unstable ground and then seeing what happens when she attempts to cope with this unstable environment. Having heard that Olivia is not receiving suits, Viola hatches the plan to put herself in the service of Orsino and 'What else may hap, to time . . . commit' (1.2.56). This is the final oath of allegiance to chance, time and contingency – perhaps the purest oath sworn in the play that is not about love – but it is also the clue that Shakespeare gives us to the nature of the process that is unfolding on stage. Viola's two declarations of waiting upon occasion show us that the dynamism carrying this play forward is one that moves in periods of encapsulation: three times Viola makes reference to her own identity, and these moments are forecast and recalled in various criss-crossing structures of inclusion. 'Who does beguile you' she says to Olivia, who expects her to reveal that the two of them are now hus-band and wife. This is exactly one of those unripe moments whose existence she has forecast in her opening speech, an occasion that bids or invites silence from the adept sworn to uphold its mysteries. (She could, after all, spill the beans about her identity now, when the matter has come to question.) But the declaration also calls attention to the spatial arrangement of bodies both literally standing on stage and, figuratively or virtually, in other rooms in the *Twelfth Night* garden. Olivia has cut through the hedge in the wrong place and taken the wrong man for her husband, the very man to whom min-utes ago she entrusted the task of revealing that they are essentially new persons with new allegiances: husband and wife. (As an entice-ment to enter the chantry with the priest, Olivia has promised the wonder-struck Sebastian that the priest will keep the secret of their marriage 'whiles you are willing it shall come to note', essentially, until you say otherwise.) What is funny about this carefully choreo-graphed confusion of identity is also what makes it revealing about the metaphysics of process: the Viola who is canny enough to point out that Olivia is literally talking *to* and *about* someone else in this scene is simultaneously (as far as Olivia is concerned) a man who is refusing to act at the right time, to seize occasion by the forelock and take on greatness at a run. The play does not fall apart at this moment, but rather *increases* its tempo, hurtling towards the real moment of

ripeness when the identically dressed twins stand face to face in front
of their prospective lovers and antagonists. The multiple circles that
have been drawn around Viola have now linked this place and
moment to others in the play where the shifting convergence of place
and moment – the reality of occasion – was explicitly set out and
affirmed, and it is that linkage that audiences think about when they
find the scene humorous. We are being given a tutorial in the immanence of theatrical substances to themselves and others, their exquisite dependence upon sets of spatial relations and future-entailing
promises. In *Twelfth Night*, this process is essentially comic: the very
mistakes that are heaped onto the situation in this scene will only
increase the value of the next, because those mistakes are a necessary
part of what follows. We can hold off on saying exactly who or what
is speaking at this moment, since the creature who asks Olivia who
precisely she is talking to is 'the one becoming Viola, who was once
Cesario'. The man she is taken for, in turn, is 'the one becoming
Sebastian, who is no longer Cesario, nor Viola'. As Whitehead would
say in a different context, 'No two actualities can be torn apart: each
is all in all' (*PR* 348).

Quite often in his work, Whitehead will offer what sounds like a
pithy aphorism in the middle of a highly technical argument, a phrase
that interrupts the reader and sets open a door to insights that may
be missing from the formal system that is being elaborated. This is
one of the reasons why it is often better to read Whitehead himself,
despite the daunting technical terms, instead of commentators who
lack his cross-cutting wit. When Whitehead says in *Process and
Reality* that 'no two actualities can be torn apart: each is all in all', we
are treated to the same metaphysical flair that is apparent in Shakespeare's 'the counterchange is severally in all'. Whitehead's statement,
of course, is meant to force readers to reflect on the paradoxical
nature of metaphysical immanence: the way in which each of his
'actual occasions', having been detached from the punctual logic of
spatially and temporally discrete substances, can now be immersed
in a mutually contrastive/inclusive structure whereby each occasion

is a part of a manifold that is itself, as manifold, present in some derivative sense in every other. Whitehead is taking two seventeenth-century philosophers, Spinoza and Leibniz, as his inspiration for this kind of gesture, but he is trying to add something of his own to this radically synthetic early modern way of thinking about wholes and parts. (Whitehead was perhaps the only seventeenth-century philosopher who managed to be born in the twentieth.) For Whitehead is also interested in something he calls creativity, an aspect or 'category of the ultimate', as he calls it, that accounts for process's ever-unfolding movement across new configurations of occasions. Just as important, he wants to assure that the utter singularity of each new actual occasion does not orphan or detach that occasion from the others it 'prehends' and those it will be 'prehended' by. Because these two ends are pursued concurrently, Whitehead's metaphysics must account for the utterly new as it emerges from what already exists (the problem of novelty), but also explain how such novelty becomes intelligible through the 'solidarity' of emerging actual occasions with all others. This is a tension that Shakespeare must reconcile as well, since in premising two of his characters' identities on a unique and unexpected occasion, he is constantly negotiating the danger that the final scene will appear so singular – so fleetingly dependent, that is, on similarly unexpected meetings and novel circumstances – that it seems to have no emotional or causal relationship with the events that have come before it and which are to follow. Occasion can be creative, as it certainly is in *Twelfth Night*, but it must work in some kind of patterned way towards intelligible, particular ends if there is to be laughter and perhaps personhood.

Whitehead's solution to the tension between novelty and solidarity involves a doctrine of 'objectification', one that refers not to some disembodied scientific perspective on things, but to a technical process whereby occasions are integrated into some kind of matrix of relation. We might think of this process as the metaphysical analogue to the dynamic process whereby past and anticipated moments of a performance are synthesized by the theatrical spectator. Such an analogy, however, really attenuates the broader continuum of processes (material causation, perception, emotional reaction, cognition) captured by Whitehead's more abstract account of 'objectification', which is why we will be avoiding this more overtly psychological language in the brief exposition that follows. For Whitehead, objectification describes the way in which particular actual occasions that must be related to one another – occasions that are being aggregated into ever larger groupings called societies or nexuses – are each, at some point in the process of concrescence, apprehended within an 'extensive continuum'. The extensive continuum is a realm of relationality so abstract that it supports references that cannot be described in any of our known geometries, much less our ordinary conception of three-dimensional space undergoing differentiation through time. I am not going to attempt to reconstruct the entire process of objectification here – it is only relevant as a window onto Shakespeare treatment of how theatrical substances come to be – but I will point out some basic dynamics in the system and some of the reasons behind Whitehead's metaphysical choices. Whitehead settles on the extended continuum because it harnesses the relational power of classes, what are essentially levels of logical generalization and inclusion, and puts that power in the service of metaphysical explanation. For example, when trying to demonstrate that change and novelty are immanent to any process of development – when trying, that is, to show how the quality and aim characterizing a given concrescing entity are generated from *within* and *throughout* its process of generation – Whitehead uses levels of inclusion and the contrasts in their contents as an engine for self-derived difference and novelty. He uses a kind of abbreviated algebra to explain this process, asking us to consider a situation in which occasion A is in the process of prehending several other actual occasions, B, C and D. Now occasion A 'feels' all of these other occasions, and in doing so is on the way to imposing its own 'subjective unity' on them, a unity that derives from the entire process of concrescence and so is its own reason for being. (We must remember here that feeling, for Whitehead, does not necessarily refer psychologically to conscious perception, but rather to a mode of relation.) But occasion A also feels entity B's feelings of C and D, since they are included in B for the feelings of A. Similarly, occasion A has access to the feelings C has of D, and to its own feeling of D alone. Now *all* of these feelings are real and thus comparable, which means that they can be contrasted in such a way that the variety of actual occasions prehended by A – here, occasion D *as felt* from the perspective of A, B and C – is scanned for inconsistencies which are eliminated in what he calls 'positive' and 'negative prehension'. Both the inclusions and the exclusions are then stamped, in effect, on the emerging actual occasion A, contributing to it a unique character or 'subjective unity'. As Whitehead says, 'A feeling bears on itself the scars of its birth . . . it retains the impress of what it might have been, but is not' (*PR*, 226–27).

One can see even from this small example taken from the process of objectification the strong imprint of Whitehead's training in logic and mathematics: the array of more and less inclusive 'sets' of feelings constituting classes of items to be set in relation to one another; the move to make contrasts within contrasts – A comparing its own feeling of D with the already contrasting feelings of D derived through B and C – which recalls the operations of integration in the calculus. What supports this vast relational apparatus is a set of recursive operations that allow elements 'captured' or 'felt but then excluded' in one stage of an entity's genesis to be compared with and then integrated into subsequent feelings in that entity's lifetime. In developing this inventory of positive and negative prehensions, the actual occasion is said to acquire 'subjective aim', a measure of conceptual unity that differentiates the occasion from within. The same dynamic of prehension, comparison and integration holds for larger metaphysical entities such as societies of actual occasions – which for Whitehead compose the 'macroscopic' entities observed in space-time such as rocks, plants and persons. Such societies, which are distinguished by a sort of genetic unity emergent in the course of generation, are capable of sustaining comparisons of their various sorts of feelings (some 'physical', some 'conceptual') and in doing so re-organizing their subjective aims, sometimes to the point of consciousness. Here too, as in the algebraic micro-scale example, quality, character, form and even desire or appetite are generated by the same process of 'creative advance' for all entities that can exist and be known. Asserting this uniformity in the *way* process works is partly what makes Whitehead a philosopher of immanence: all becoming everywhere is of the same type; it does not require a 'special kind' of actor working on another 'kind' of stuff. Something like a scalable metaphysics results, for it follows that *any* given entity or occasion – whether that entity is an abstract idea, a rock, the perception of the colour red, a feeling of hunger – is to be understood with respect to the other actual occasions or societies that make up its environment or background. And while many of those 'other actual occasions' occurred in the past, the pastness of the past is no obstacle to the process of objectification. Perished or 'satisfied' actual occasions are objectified for eternity in God, who has, as one part of his formal nature, the job of conserving or 'saving' the disappearing world of actual occasions for subsequent processes of objectification.

Such a complicated flux of becoming has to occur somewhere, and that somewhere is the most universal 'level' of Whitehead's system: not God, but the extensive continuum. The extensive continuum is the realm in which actual entities assume all possible forms of relation, whether they are relations of inclusion, integration, relation, spatial and temporal differentiation and so on. Metaphysically speaking, the extensive continuum is one of Whitehead's most exotic creations, and it is the one that is going to lead us back to the particular metaphysics of *Twelfth Night* when we return to the play in a moment. According to Whitehead, the extensive continuum is:

> one relational complex in which all potential objectifications find their niche . . . An extensive continuum is a complex of entities united by the various allied relationships of whole to part, and of overlapping so as to possess common parts, and of contact, and of

other relationships derived from these primary relationships . . . [it] expresses the solidarity of all possible standpoints throughout the whole process of the world. (*PR*, 66)

The continuum is one, a metaphysical plenum that can support atomistic events or occasions precisely because it exhausts the modes of relation we think of as part to whole, inclusion, exclusion and overlap. That continuum is more real than geometry, space and time, in comparison with which all three of the latter are derivative abstractions. (To mistake space and time as given or fundamental phenomena, as Whitehead notes many natural philosophers of the seventeenth century did, is to commit the fallacy of 'misplaced concreteness'.) Increasing the level of abstraction does what it always does in Whitehead: it offers new ways of accounting for the solidarity of elements that can now be understood as both ontologically distinct (by virtue of the relations they uniquely configure and actually own) and intrinsically relatable (by virtue of their joint inclusion within a larger level). One does not have to be convinced of the truth of this metaphysical scheme to grasp the basic impulse here, as well as the consequences for the kinds of metaphysical entities one is willing to entertain.

Ultimately, it is the raw generality of Whitehead's concept of the extensive continuum as a medium of becoming – its ability to call attention to relatedness in a *minimal* sense not available in other discursive or logical contexts – that helps us to grasp the buoyant quality of the final reunion that Shakespeare has enacted on stage. The play begins by linking the essential aspects of a character's identity to a shifting logjam of circumstance called 'occasion', and then proceeds to enclose important potential revelations (Viola's identity, the facts of Olivia's marriage) within restricted populations of the play's characters. By dramaturgically intersplicing the entrance and exits of these characters into and out of a spatial receptacle (the stage) that is *itself* moving through different 'rooms' in the play – rooms that characters cannot differentiate on the basis of their contents because the same 'person' (Viola/Sebastian) can be in two places at once – the play paces its characters towards the final moment when an individual's identity finally begins to coalesce. This final stage of coalescence represents a late stage of 'becoming' in the play's array of theatrical substances, substances that only come into being in and through the series of events that relate them to one another. The technical trick of *Twelfth Night*, dramaturgically speaking, is thus that it manages to enclose the events that constitute its characters – the premature collections or intersections of stage actors in moments that are not quite 'ripe' – into ever more inclusive structures of dependence, so that the occasion that constitutes the ultimate stepping-into-being of its two principal actors actually *comprehends* much of the previous action in the play. The being of theatrical substance, or the thickness of identity in the world of these speaking entities on stage, is thus, in Whiteheadean terms, a process of 'objectification' in which elements of past forms of relation and feeling are summed up or integrated into new and more inclusive structures of relation and comprehension. Whitehead has a phrase for this quality: 'novel togetherness'.

* * *

The final goal of *Twelfth Night*, then, is the production of a wondrous form of novelty, an event so singular that it both defines its contents utterly while simultaneously creating a meaningful relationship between its contents and those of events that preceded it. This is a real theatrical goal and accomplishment, not just a metaphysical point that Shakespeare is scoring in the outer reaches of set theory. For what happens when this kind of novel togetherness is created on stage is that the meaning of togetherness – both as a phenomenal fact of bodies on stage or in the theatre, and as a feature of the plot as characters 'meet' – has a metaphysical status that is inseparable from its emotional content. Why is it thrilling to hear Viola and Sebastian narrate, at arms length, the details of their parentage, their shared history, with only gradual introduction of their separation in the storm and their slow reconciliation by mishap and cross-adventure? Because it is so clear that their belonging together at this moment – and so, their mutual differentiation – is a completely immanent form of interrelation. Whitehead has helped us to understand what this term might mean, since Whiteheadean immanence requires occasion to supply its own native logic, an origin of character that both inherits and adds to the past without reaching out to some transcendent agent to direct things from the outside. Certainly the lack of outside direction is apparent in the *Twelfth Nigh*: unlike *Hamlet*, where contingency and providence are closely linked, *Twelfth Night* works out its ending *without* enclosing its own action in the rhetorical shell of God's invisible governance. Indeed, what Shakespeare would have been thinking about as he plotted out the events of *Twelfth Night* was probably the mishaps of his earlier comedies – *The Comedy of Errors*, for instance – which are short on transcendence and instead puffed along in a series of micro-climates that seem to change from scene to scene. The full significance of Shakespeare's affirmation of immanence, in fact, depends on the rich structure of accidental intersection and successive comprehension that takes shape throughout the play, a process Viola can only wonder about when she asks midway through the play, 'How will this fadge?' (2.2.31) Such a principle of construction embodies, in a different register, the logical strategy of successive encapsulation and inclusion that characterizes Whitehead's metaphysical work. The difference is that where Whitehead ends with universal categories such as the extensive continuum – his grounding domain of pure and therefore *mere* relation – Shakespeare's largest container is the physical domain of performance itself. Everyone watching the final scene finds him or herself in the last and largest room of the garden, the one in which meaning, identity and feeling are a product of relations (and relationality) rather than the local sources of agency embodied in this or that actor on stage.

There is something deeply pleasurable about finding oneself present to the actors in the same way that the actors are present to each other, in occupying the same container and thus being the same kind of thing – the contents of an event – that is unfolding around you. It is this form of novel togetherness that is the metaphysical ideal and emotional destination of *Twelfth Night*, and it is the one that the play works deliberately to unfold in plot, language and action. But the play is also illustrating the binding or integrating power of immanent inclusion in smaller ways as well, for example in its depiction of the process whereby novelty emerges as a form of comic error. The fooling of Malvolio and humorous exchanges that take place around Andrew Aguecheek are all illustrative here. Malvolio, of course, is another adept of fortune—'Tis but fortune, all is fortune', he declares as he takes the stage in act 2 – although he is really fortune's victim rather than its darling. In the hilarious garden scene (2.5) where Maria gulls Malvolio with the spurious love letter, we see a perfect example of how process can unfold its own immanent meanings without the direct external direction of anyone. Shakespeare has already given the audience a clue about the self-unfolding nature of the mayhem that is going to occur in this scene when it is hatched two scenes earlier (2.3). Having told Toby and Andrew about her plan to imitate her mistress's handwriting, she tells them:

> *Mar.* I will plant you two – and let the fool make a third – where he shall find the letter. Observe his construction of it. For this night, to bed, and dream on the event. Farewell.
>
> (2.3.153–55)

The word 'event' here, as discussed above, refers to the outcome of a process that cannot be directly handled, but which comes about through the cooperation of circumstance. Maria is saying that Malvolio will 'construct' or interpret the ambiguous letter as an invitation to him from his mistress to courtship: this is the plan. But she is also making reference to something like the 'container trick' that Shakespeare is going to work in the last scene, referring to a famous early modern image that depicted two persons and bore the title

'Three Fools'. (The third was the viewer.) Like the painting that her comment recalls, like the garden that encloses the various groups of actors, and like the theatre that will ultimately enclose and comprehend the audience and actors, the plot that Maria is launching is really a container for a kind of self-actualizing creativity that can incorporate anything in its path.

It should be no surprise, then, that the 'obstructions' (2.5.106) to Malvolio's egotistical interpretation of the letter are, if anything, a spur to ever more extravagant fantasy. Reading the abbreviation for the addressee of the letter, M.O.I.A., and asking himself if they refer to him, Malvolio proceeds to take the sequence and 'crush it a little' in order to find his name secreted inside. His delight in finding himself 'named' in the love letter – his premature grasping at novel togetherness with his mistress, we might say – proves that process is omnivorous: it overwhelms anything in its path because the creativity that pushes process forward will always make use of what is before it. In fact, however, Malvolio does not understand occasion and process at all, his protestations about fortune notwithstanding. Malvolio believes in the real substance of character – he tells Toby, for example, to 'separate yourself and your misdemeanors' (2.3.87–88) – and, unlike Viola, he refuses to wait on the 'jump' of circumstances before 'revealing' his identity as Olivia's beloved. The irony of the situation is that at the very moment when Malvolio thinks he has taken fortune or occasion by the forelock, he has really become the pawn of someone else. Toby, Maria and Andrew are laughing at him precisely because they see how automatic certain types of confusion really are: once the bait has been dangled – Whitehead might refer to Maria's letter as a 'lure for feeling' – the situation itself conspires to lead Malvolio farther and farther upstream. The bad *kairos* that characterizes Malvolio's situation will, in fact, continue to generate its effects as love turns automatically to unrelieved bitterness once the plot is exposed, Malvolio sliding irreversibly into the perfectly awful drama of humiliation that awaits him. Occasion will give birth to brother and sister in the case of Sebastian and Viola; in the case of Malvolio, the final scene promises differentiation of another sort, something more like exile into a hinterland of revenge that is no more avoidable than the twins' joy in their new circumstances. He has become the 'scar', as Whitehead might say, that occasion must bear as the mark of its birth.

The Malvolio subplot presents audiences with a miniature version of process and its coalescence around events that Shakespeare is unfolding for the audience throughout the course of the play as a whole. True, the contingency or eventuality of 'occasion' in the play is an illusion of the dramatist's craft: there is always a sense in which audiences are not really witnessing process in its utter spontaneity and self-generating power, since Shakespeare the dramatist has set things up in advance. But the audience of *Twelfth Night* is, like the conspirators in the bushes, shown how situations can plausibly *generate* particular types of outcomes that no individual him or herself could bring about alone. (No one would laugh if the letter simply said, 'I, Olivia, love you, Malvolio'.) We find humour, that is, in the automatic collation of elements that have been placed in a certain kind of container that relates them to one another together: in a garden, a text, a space on the stage. Such powers of automatic integration and differentiation are really the essence of occasion and, in a sense, the key to its creative advancing power; *mere* relation is its hidden, tensile strength, the wispy circle of inclusion that it can draw around any group of agents. Even dialogue can be included in such a container, which we learn from the back and forth exchanges between Andrew and Toby. When Sir Andrew first arrives to greet Sir Toby, the two men exchange pleasantries and then turn their attention to Maria, who is standing alongside Toby when Andrew arrives. Toby urges Andrew on to bold courtship in an early appearance of one of the play's key themes:

> Enter Sir Andrew [Aguecheek]
> *Sir And.* Sir Toby Belch! How now, Sir Toby Belch?
> *Sir Toby.* Sweet Sir Andrew.

> *Sir And.* [to Maria]: Bless you, fair shrew.
> *Maria.* And you too, sir.
> *Sir Toby.* Accost, Sir Andrew, accost.
> *Sir And.* What's that?
> *Sir Toby.* My niece's chambermaid.
> *Sir And.* Good Mistress Accost, I desire better acquaintance.
> *Maria.* My name is Mary, sir.
> *Sir And.* Good Mistress Mary Accost.

(1.3.37–46)

How, one wonders, could one manage to create a line as odd and silly as 'Good Mistress Mary Accost' in any organic fashion? The answer is, get the right people together in the right places, and let the situation do its work. Andrew thinks Maria is giving him her Christian name, while Maria is attempting to clear up the confusion, an attempt that is then recycled into more confusion. We are back to the algebraic scene of Whiteheadean objectification here, where the results of one prehension (Mistress Accost) are integrated with another (Mary). The result is novel mayhem, but also a demonstration of the way in which the recitation or enactment of a contingent sequence of events (as in my quotation of the serial misprision above) becomes, from a Whiteheadean perspective, an illustration of the fact that it is *mere* relation that is doing the integrating and, so, metaphysical work in a given situation. Action and analysis become interchangeable in such a scene, since beyond occasion – itself the beginning and end of knowledge – there is nothing more to describe or understand.

The final scene of *Twelfth Night* is its own novel kind of mayhem, but of course it is much more serious than the verbal mistakings of Sir Andrew. Perhaps what makes it especially complex is the sheer connectivity of its geometry: the last scene of the play is structured around a multitude of entrances, all of which add further consequence to the ultimate meeting that occurs when Sebastian arrives at line 200. First there are Feste and Fabian joking with one another, then the Duke and Viola arrive to banter with the fool. After the fool leaves, Antonio arrives with the officers and his past conflict with Orsino is rehearsed, along with the first hints of Sebastian's survival, since Antonio claims to have spent the preceding three months with him. Next comes Olivia, who reveals that Cesario is her 'husband' and produces a priest (right on time) to prove it. As Orsino is berating Cesario/Viola for his disloyalty, Sir Andrew arrives and accuses Viola of having attacked him and Sir Toby, the latter arriving with Feste only to be dismissed to a surgeon. Each arrival brings another piece of the play's business to the table, linking the quarrels of the characters to each other like pages sewn together in a quire. It is important to rehearse the sequence of entrances here because the play's strategy of inclusion requires nearly the entire cast to assemble on stage before Sebastian makes his entrance. Significantly, we can only explain the mechanics of this final scene – the *how* of its unfolding – by serially redescribing the events *as they happen* on stage. Shakespearean metaphysics has become adverbial, and this is our clue to the fact that we are dealing with a truly novel occasion: like the joke 'Mistress Mary Accost', the meaning of this final scene depends on circumstances being a certain way, and the only way to communicate what that way is to set out the circumstances as they occurred – to diagram the situation, which in this cases means pointing to the play itself. And because the relationship of the elements in this diagram, on the living stage, is an immanent one, it cannot be reduced to a formula or boiled down with some kind of causal shorthand. Rather, this happened, and then this happened; meanwhile this was going on, and this and this. The diagram moves, because it must.

We have arrived at the final moment of gathering, which at this point must be both organically productive and singularly unprompted – a mere coming together that is nevertheless full of consequence. Olivia's husband first greets Antonio but then turns to see what all others are seeing as the last partition is removed: himself, or another version of himself. 'Do I stand there?' (5.1.219) Sebastian asks, laying out the paradox of the encounter in its most hyperbolic form. The point of this final scene, if what I am saying about

Shakespeare's metaphysics is correct, is not to show characters emerging out of the welter of criss-crossed circumstances in order to become self-sufficient substances, eliminating, in effect, the second 'I' that stands before Sebastian as a taunt or wonder. Rather, it is to show that both the characters and the events that unite them – our theatrical substances and the accidents that befall them – are part of the same immanent reality, neither trumping the other in terms of its metaphysical priority. Sebastian is *in* this final occasion, just as the occasion is *in* Sebastian: all are part of a single society whose genetic history gives it its particular character and what Whitehead, in a text entitled *Adventures in Ideas*, calls 'affective tone' (*AI*, 178). What is appealing about the scene dramatically is the way in which that particular tonality, comic and wondrous as it is, seems to be generated from within the scene itself. If one were to write out longhand the conditions that have been satisfied by this reunion scene and then ask what would need to happen to produce *this* particular outcome, we would have to copy out the play itself as it progresses to this point. The scene's self-sufficiency in a metaphysical sense comes from its utter novelty, from its status (to adapt a phrase of Sebastian's) as an 'accident' that 'exceed[s] all instance' (4.3.11–12). And yet, if we say that everything that went before it was relevant to the creation of this scene, we might also say that nothing was, because once the encounter between the twins has taken place, all of the previous relationships are immediately integrated into something new.

If there is a philosophical personality that the play offers up for emulation, I suspect it does not belong to a character on stage, but to the audience member who balances Sebastian and Viola as parts of a contrastive, gradually intensifying whole. Sebastian marvels at the strange circumstances he encounters in Illyria – 'This is the air, that is the glorious sun' (4.3.1) – but he does not dismiss them as mere sensory babble. Dramaturgically, he represents a principle of embodied reaction, an empirical consciousness waiting to be unleashed on the scene in the final act. Viola, on the other hand, is a principle of potential or deferred action (perhaps even duration), navigating the world with guile and subtlety until occasion ripens to the point where secrets can be revealed. One is physics, the other metaphysics. Neither is the master of process, but both are crucial parts of it. Both are part of something omnivorous as well, the great comprehending power of extension and its ability to offer up the world in parts that can be circled, chunked and nested into ever greater aggregates or societies of reality. Shakespeare is quite aware of this omnivorous quality of reality – it is the hallmark of comic misconstruction, and beyond this, desire – and he calls attention to it earlier in the play through a sly remark by Feste. Commenting on Orsino's changeable, melancholic mind, Feste says:

> Now the melancholy god protect thee, and the tailor make thy doublet of changeable taffeta, for thy mind is a very opal. I would have men of such constancy put to sea, that their business might be everything, and their intent everywhere, for that's it that always makes a good voyage of nothing'. (2.4.71–76)

The sea, which is where the first accident that began the play occurred, is capable of supporting travel in any direction: so much the better if the person it carries has no fixed desire of his own, for he will always be satisfied with the result. The quality Feste assigns to individuals like Orsino, having any business anywhere (while thinking he is pursuing one business somewhere), is exactly the one that Shakespeare reserves for his most dramatic event in the conclusion. Like taffeta, which can show colors whose complexity defies the simple weave of threads, or the aimless sailor who is pleased with whatever happens, comic process can always make a 'good voyage of nothing'. Or rather, can make something of nothing. Novelty is the fruit of togetherness, a quality that depends upon occasion's inclusiveness of the past but also that special something that occasion adds of its own to itself. Whitehead puts it this way: 'The world expands through recurrent unifications of itself, each, by the addition of itself, automatically recreating the multiplicity anew' (*PR*, 286). Shakespeare has a similar metaphysical intuition into process, but gives it a theatrical exposition and a comic flavour, pacing the movement of his characters to the spiraling rhythms of the 'whirligig of time'. When Feste sings his final song about the 'great while ago' when 'the world begun', he concludes in the final stanza 'that's all one, our play is done', testifying to the indifferent inclusiveness of comic resolution and the capacious occasion of performance itself. This is precisely the creativity and immanent unity that Shakespeare would tear apart when he turned to the nothing of *King Lear*.

Chapter 3

Lear's Intensity, Bergson's Divided Kingdom

When the curtain opens on *Lear*, we are thrust into a very different world, one in which immanence is no longer a characteristic of comic inclusion and satisfaction but, rather, a mark of exile from a kingdom that will not tolerate its incalculable emotional possibilities and costs. We notice the contrast immediately when we compare Lear's posture towards the volatility of occasion with that of Viola, who in *Twelfth Night* seems always to be waiting for that ripe moment in which circumstances have conspired to assist action. Lear does just the opposite, and in the manufactured 'occasion' of the love contest with which the play opens, we see him attempting to do what Viola manages consistently to avoid doing throughout the earlier comedy: he reveals all to everyone, and in so doing attempts to cancel any further dependence on occasion for the remainder of his life (crawling 'unburdened' to 'death'). Instead of giving away his lands and his responsibilities, however, Lear makes himself a permanent dependent on the generosity and fiat of others. The plan to outsmart fortune has gone badly wrong, and there is something about Lear's refusal to wait – his feeling that occasion can be manufactured just as love can be forced to speak on command – that is both ghastly and revealing when compared with Viola's patience and indirection. Indeed, the last remnants of any sense of beneficial spontaneity disappear from Lear's world the moment his youngest daughter fails to please him. The 1623 First Folio version of the play registers this fatal disruption of Lear's staged divestiture in a halting exchange of the word 'nothing':

> *Lear.* . . . what can you say to draw
> A third more opulent than your sisters? Speak.
>
> *Cord.* Nothing, my lord.
> *Lear.* Nothing?
>
> *Cord.* Nothing.
> *Lear.* Nothing will come of nothing. Speak again.
> (1.1.83–88)

By the time we get to the fifth 'nothing' in this sequence, there can be no doubt about the change that has occurred in the quality of time: the goddess of 'occasion' that ruled *Twelfth Night* has turned her back on this scene. In comparison with *Lear*, there is a creativity and digestive openness in the comic world of *Twelfth Night* that allows 'a good voyage' to be made 'of nothing', for 'all' to become 'one' and then another 'one' to appear on the horizon, just as new, just as susceptible to incorporation in the temporal stream. In *The Tragedy of King Lear*, as the First Folio version was called, time becomes an almost indifferent medium – uncoaxable, as it were – with a thickness that grips its contents so tightly they cannot move. Loving daughters refuse to speak. Messengers fail to arrive at their destinations in time. Orders countermanding executions do not get delivered. Nothing will come of nothing, Lear says. So too, new words cease to arrive when the time of ceremonial exchange has halted. As Lear tries helplessly to put the verbal thread back into the needle that has been drawing events along, he cites a cosmological commonplace (nothing will come from nothing, *ex nihilo nihil fit*) in the middle of an echo-chamber. Time has lost its sympathetic sense, and occasion appears to have gone on strike.

The idea that one could somehow rewind the time of a discussion – that *one* time might be as good as *another* as a container for events – is full of metaphysical consequence, and seems to be part of a deeper fascination with quantity and interchangeability in *Lear*. One does not have to look far through the text of either version of the play to notice the almost gratuitous emphasis on the specificities of number. The disguised Edgar, playing Poor Tom, has 'three suits to his back, six shirts to his body' and once rode a 'bay trotting-horse over four-inched bridges' (3.4.120–21; 53–54); the fool teaches Kent in rhyme how to have 'more /Than two tens to a score' (1.4.112–13); Lear goes to Dover with 35 or 36 knights after having wrangled laboriously with his daughters over the quantity of his train (3.7.14); his heart will 'break into a hundred thousand flaws' before he will weep (2.2.450); Cordelia sends a 'century' (100 men) to look for her father around Dover (4.3.6); Lear's age is 'Fourscore and upward, / Not an hour more nor less' (4.6.54–55).

The proliferation of quantities in *Lear* resonates with its thematic concerns, something we will discuss in a moment, but it does so on the level of textual revision and performance as well. In a fine study of Shakespeare's work as a reviser of his own texts, John Jones has argued that in handling the detail about Lear's age, the 1623 First Folio edition of the text – altered, many scholars believe, in light of theatrical performance – shows Shakespeare adding 'Not an hour more nor less' to the already vague 'Fourscore and upward' from the earlier 1608 Quarto text. (The 1608 Quarto has been named the First Quarto because it was followed by a second that appeared in 1619; we will only be dealing with the so-called 'First Quarto' of 1608 and the 'First Folio' of 1623 in our analysis.) Such a seemingly absurd revision in the Folio *Lear* suggests to Jones that Shakespeare's interest in numbers and quantity in this play was so intimate, so fussy, that it provides one of the most vivid glimpses we may ever have into the playwright's mind and style. Such revisions or textual 'variants' are so gratuitous or 'transcendental' (179), as he puts it, that they are purely stylistic, momentary or occasional, the marks of an artist working on the fly and heeding impulses we cannot hope to reconstruct. Jones is right, I think, in saying that Shakespeare was deeply fascinated by the power of number in this play, and correct too in arguing that we may never be able to explain some of his revisionary fiddling with its sprawling math. (While we can never be certain of the precise role that Shakespeare played in making these changes found in the Folio *Lear* – scholars still debate precisely how these source texts came to exist in their differing forms – the remarkable clustering of alterations specifically around matters of quantity and repetition suggest an interested authorial mind at work in such instances.) But the intimacy of Shakespeare's choices should not obscure for us the metaphysical insight that was driving Shakespeare to play with *specific* numbers, to put them out on stage and think aloud about how quantity and repetition might effect our perception of things, persons and events in the theatre. What, metaphysically speaking, is the effect of giving Tom six shirts or changing the exact age of Lear, or even of letting an audience hear the hanging word 'never' five times in Lear's exchange with Cordelia rather than the three times specified in the First Quarto edition of the play, where Lear does not ask her to repeat her answer? In making these changes, Shakespeare provided his audience (and perhaps himself) with an opportunity to think deliberately about the power of number to be specific – to provide measurements of something – regardless of the real object that it refers to. The strange power of nothing to measure something is brought into focus in a telling exchange between Lear and the fool before Albany's castle. 'The reason why the seven stars are no more than seven is a pretty reason', (1.5.31–32) the fool tells Lear in an extended exchange of riddles. Lear answers, 'Because they are not eight', and in doing so, points out the utterly arbitrary nature of numerical definitions and measurements of things.

But the cognitive and poetic appeal of quantity cannot be explained with a tautology. Numbers are not effective or descriptive because quantities differ, but because the hypothetical continuum of differing quantities allows one to make comparisons among things that would otherwise be incomparable. Ask yourself why Lear's heart threatens to break into a number of fragments 1000 times as great as the number of men Cordelia sends to recover him, and you begin to see the limits of purely numerical comparisons. Here, in his attention to what we might call the gratuitous sense of numbers, is where Shakespeare's interest in numbers and the larger thematic concerns of the play – most obviously, its acidic view of the quantitative meaning of age and the quality of wisdom it is supposed to confer – begin to overlap with the philosophical concerns of Henri Bergson. For Bergson, it was the job of metaphysics to clarify the meaning of both quantity and quality, two absolutely fundamental categories that are widely misunderstood in discussions of perception and events in the natural world. In perhaps his most focused exploration of this topic, a text entitled *Time and Free Will*, Bergson argues for a divided kingdom within metaphysics, with quantitative reasoning operating in the realm of received, practical or utilitarian consciousness and a vastly different, qualitative realm reserved for a dreamlike, but also more fundamental, mode of perception that the quantitative mode organizes and occasionally usurps. For Bergson, who was trained as a mathematician and, like Whitehead, was conversant in contemporary developments in the sciences, any act of quantification implied the spatialization of time, perception and memory. This meant that one assumed a kind of interchangeability of times and comparability of all quantities – time being an empty container, something to be filled, refilled or refreshed – on the grounds that both time and space were indifferently extended media, stretching out from one point and reaching towards another. But we would be wrong to believe that changes in the quantity of something, quantity being something that can be increased or diminished, would result in a parallel increase or decrease in the magnitude of a particular quality. A long silence is not a shorter one raised to a higher degree of power. It is actually a different kind of silence. Individual qualities never 'scale' up or down in the same way that quantities do; they simply become other, different qualities (*this* silence), suggesting that it is their internally diversifying power – as opposed to quantity's extensive, additive nature – that make qualities unique in Bergson's analysis. Does Lear's soul have parts, 'flaws' or fragments that could be counted? Would its shattering into 100,000 parts be 10,000 times worse than its fragmentation into 100? Yes, of course, but surely also – no. Bergson would look at Lear's statement with the same sense of irony Shakespeare appears to have felt when adding 'not an hour more nor less' to Lear's 'fourscore and upward' years. The number is meaningful in its inapplicability, for the age of Lear and, thus, his *quality* of being wise or a fool are changing with every moment of the play. The shattering he imagines would be a different experience – and he, consequentially, an entirely different being – if the pieces of his soul numbered 100,001.

Bergson's account of the non-scalability of individual qualities, the way they multiply in kind whenever we try to 'increase' or 'decrease' them in some quantitative sense, designates what for him is a specific domain of reality and experience which he argues cannot be measured, mathematicized or accommodated by the spatializing techniques of practical action. This domain, which he calls 'duration', is what is really real in the world, constituted as it is by a great multiplicity of sensations or interactions that mix and overlap with one another without being entirely separable into spatially or temporally discrete units. Something of this capacity for flux, which Bergson locates at a fundamentally pre-practical level of consciousness, also underlies the political landscape of *Lear*. The institution of kingship, for example, which normally locates the principle of political order at the top of a social pyramid, has suddenly become a polygon with an incalculable number of sides. Political loyalties, filial duties, even the geographical emanation of family power from an ancient seat are no longer keyed to the triangular principals of point projection. (Why, for example, do Regan and Cornwall exercise their power from Gloucester's estate?) Punctualism and the institutions of patriarchy and monarchy that it anchors are losing their purchase: that quality of good, buoyant immanence we saw in the final scene of *Twelfth Night* has now become the bad immanence – at least for Jacobean audiences – of power scattering mercurially around new centres of control. Where there was one king, there are now two. Where the old were assumed to be wise and fit for command, we now have greybeards who act like children. Where love and land seemed interchangeable, subject to the quantitative physics of balance or measure, we have the heaving tug-of-war of dynastic conflict, provisional alliances betrayed as the eddies of power surface, move and reappear. A score no longer contains two tens. And in the midst of this dramatized image of the horses bolting from the paddock, we have Shakespeare counting aloud to himself, thinking about just what it is that *accumulates* in experience and how such accumulation can be understood if it cannot be counted, compounded or compared.

Both the 1608 First Quarto and 1623 First Folio editions of *Lear*, or rather, the parallax difference between the two, place us in a position similar to the one in which Bergson stood when he began to ask his most compelling questions about time, space and the qualities of experience. For Bergson, some of the most important insights into the difference between quality and quantity were to be gained from thinking about change and motion. Thinking about the path of a shooting star, for example, Bergson notices a difference between the movement of the star itself and the places it occupies successively in its path (111). How far does it move, and is the *measure* of that motion an index of our felt perception of the bright object's flight? The mobility of the star, he says, is what is most real – what is at the root of the perception – while the path of the star, essentially an extended line drawn through space, is an abstraction. What would we have to do in order to grasp the star's mobility as such, without confusing that primary quality with the effects of such mobility (its successive occupation of locales)? Or better, given that we *do* grasp the star's mobility with a definiteness and vividness that arrests our attention, how might we preserve this essentially qualitative apprehension – an apprehension that Bergson says must take place in a state of pure 'duration' – instead of freezing each frame of the experience and mapping it onto a pinprick in space? When we strip away the mechanistic scaffolding of the world that organizes our language and perception into a spatialized set of quantities or line segments in space, we are left with the pure qualities or 'intensities' that are apprehended in consciousness. We are left, that is, with the qualitative difference between seven stars instead of eight or between seeing with one eye instead of two.

The word intensive can be confusing, although etymologically we are given a clue to its meaning from its implied contrast with 'extensive' – the latter meaning spread out or stretched over space. Taking our cue from Bergson, who associates intensity with moments of pure duration in a consciousness that *has not yet* subordinated its perceptions to spatial patterning, we might say that an intensity is something that cannot be divided or augmented and remain itself. One of Bergson's most compelling illustrations of intensity is taken from the realm of music, where units of quantity are strung together in rhythms and where intervals of tonal distance are arrayed between notes. Thinking once again about mobility, he writes:

> If consciousness is aware of anything more than positions, the reason is that it keeps the successive positions in mind and synthesizes them. But how does it carry out a synthesis of this kind? It cannot be by a fresh setting out of these same positions in a homogeneous medium, for a fresh synthesis would be necessary to connect the positions with one another, and so on indefinitely. We are thus compelled to admit that we have here to do with a synthesis which is, so to speak, qualitative, a gradual organization of our successive sensations, a unity resembling that of a phrase in a melody. This is just the idea of motion which we form when we think of it by itself, when, so to speak, from motion we extract mobility. (111)

When we think about the first four notes of Beethoven's Fifth Symphony, we are, if properly trained, fully capable of measuring out certain quantitative relationships between each note. The tonal interval between the two notes is a major third, for example, while the first three notes of da-da-da duuummm are eighth note triplets, with the longer final note counting as a half note with a fermata (which allows the orchestra conductor to extend the length given to this note to whatever she likes). Yet every time the opening phrase of the symphony is played, Bergson might argue, it has a different quality, because the proportions in the rhythm are slightly different and consciousness must synthesize the entire phrase *as a whole*. A particularly stern conductor might hold the last note for a long time, giving the opening phrase a sense of urgency or resolution. A single quality of 'urgency' does not 'increase' as the note is sustained or lengthened, however, because the phrase is not like a line segment that can be extended in 'magnitude'. Rather, the meaning or intensity of the lengthening note changes at each moment of its duration, and is equally dependent on the lengths given to the three notes preceding it. The phrase is grasped in duration by consciousness in its entirety, as an intensity. Its particular tonal feeling is immanent to every part, rather than projected from a single point in the melody.

Now think about the phenomenon of age. In the culture that Shakespeare was writing for, most of the privileges of governance and decision-making were reserved for men who were well into their natural lifespan, creating a society that at least one social historian has called a 'gerontocracy'. It was during this period, in fact, when numerical age became an important measure of one's progress through life, numbers coming to provide precision to a concept of human development that was usually measured with qualified nouns such as infant, child, adolescent, stripling, boy, girl, wench or maid. Age in this patriarchal society, moreover, was widely presumed to confer wisdom, a quality that is mentioned frequently in *Lear* and contrasted readily with the quality of foolishness, which is thought to belong to children and madmen. In their back and forth exchange in front of Albany castle in 1.5, this apparent linkage is commented on by Lear's fool. 'Thou shouldst not have been old till thou hadst been wise' (1.5.39–40), the fool says, following the larger pattern in *Lear* in which particularly important lines are delivered in monosyllabic words. The monosyllables add pauses and thus lengthen the line, providing audiences with a crucial insight into Lear's dilemma – a musical *meno mosso* in the dialogue, perhaps – at just the moment when Lear begins to contemplate the possibility that he is mad. (His very next line is 'O, let me not be mad, not mad, sweet heaven' – an almost perfect echo of the fool's monosyllables.) Age, like the length of a spoken line, acquires different qualities when apprehended as an integrated whole: each addition of a 'beat' or pause, month or year, creates a different being. Bergson recognizes this proliferation of qualities that are confused or hidden when they are keyed punctually to changes in locale or extension, arguing that:

> feeling itself is a being which lives and develops and is therefore constantly changing; otherwise how could it gradually lead us to form a resolution? Our resolution would be immediately taken. But it lives because the duration in which it develops is a duration whose moments permeate one another. By separating these moments from each other, by spreading out time in space, we have caused this feeling to lose its life and color. (133)

What Bergson is saying here is that subjective feelings are by nature processual and progressive: they move like a musical phrase that gradually accumulates meaning and emotional resonance, but the feelings themselves have a specific quality that is always changing from one moment to the next as each new sensation arrives to augment the whole. For Bergson, duration implies a 'qualitative multiplicity' of sensations and perceptions, which is to say, a multiplicity that has *not* been laid out on the ground like soldiers on a parade ground. (The latter would be a 'homogeneous' or 'quantitative multiplicity', 121). Intensity is experienced on and from the ground, in the midst of flux. For Bergson it is crucial that such intensities not be misrecognized as an 'increase' or 'decrease' in static terms like redness, sternness, mobility, grace – all words we give to perceptions that are really synthesized in the welter of duration. Instead of belonging to a person, our distinguishing qualities gather and change around us like a harmonic progression, diverted into a plurality of forms by the addition of each new note and chord.

Age in general, then, and particularly age as it appears in *Lear*, turns out to be a particularly important 'intensity' in the Bergsonian sense, one that Shakespeare suggests can be misunderstood when treated quantitatively – as a function of biological years. The Middle Ages and Renaissance recognized the 'Seven Ages of Man', a scheme rehearsed by Jacques in *As You Like It* (2.7) when he divides human development into discrete stages with identifying traits (the 'mewling, puking' child, the 'wise saws' of the justice from the fifth age). Bergson would probably say that there are as many ages as there are moments in life to synthesize: the accumulation of experience in duration multiplies the number of qualities that can be applied to that experience rather than the aggregate intensity of that experience reckoned on a single scale. Supposing that this metaphysical insight is correct, the relationship between quantities of years, say, and qualities of character (wisdom, foolishness, gravity, lightness) is not assured in some strict, linear equation. If you lengthen out a life long enough, a sage man will turn again into a child – what Jacques, in his characterization of the seventh and final age of man, calls 'second childishness' (2.2.164). This is precisely the complaint of Lear's daughters, who argue that he is behaving 'wantonly' and 'foolishly', setting up an obvious contrast between his numerical age ('four score and upward, not and hour more or less') and the quality of wisdom that is supposed to accompany his ripeness of years. Lear himself is aware, even at the height of his fury, that age and wisdom, quantity and quality, do not map onto each other reliably. 'They flattered me like a dog, and told me I had the white hairs in my beard ere the black ones were there' (4.5.95–97). Taken literally, Lear is saying that his daughters called him wise before he even had a beard, when he was still a *child*. (The acquisition of secondary sexual characteristics marked the end of childhood for boys in this period.) He is a son again, dependent on his daughters – 'childed' by them, as Edgar says in the First Quarto – and reduced to playing a game of 'handy-dandy' as he waits near Dover (4.5.144–45), comparing justice in the world to a trifle hidden in a child's hand for a game of chance.

Yet Lear is also a monarch, and the play returns obsessively to questions of how kingliness might be measured – in terms of land, men in one's train, wealth, obedience of subjects. Can a kingdom be divided in two and still be a kingdom? Can a king give away some of his substance, or all of it, and remain a king? How much, precisely, can he give away? When Lear begins to wonder about the nature of human need and poverty, finding his own feelings reflected in the bare 'unaccommodated man' (3.4.95–96), he finds new ways of apprehending his being in terms that do justice to its real, immeasurable complexity. The music of thunder seems to be the ideal soundtrack for the growing apprehension of intensity in Lear the character and *Lear* the play. (Did Shakespeare count the seconds between claps?) By the time he has been transported to Dover, encountering Gloucester who can only 'see him feelingly', there is something deadly serious about Lear's measurement of himself:

> *Glouc.* The trick of that voice I do well remember.
> Is't not the King?
> *Lear.* Ay, every inch a king.

> (4.5.103–04)

Although Lear seems to have lost some of his visible substance – the grand retinue, the crown, his court – there is another quality that can be 'seen' or apprehended through the 'trick' of the voice. Unmeasured yet qualitatively distinct, Lear becomes an indivisible monarch whose unseen inches now signify the scope of his mortality rather than the extent of his power. His own accumulated experience is now better reckoned with intensive magnitudes and relative comparison – 'I am a man / More sinned against than sinning' (3.2.58–59) – than with specific measures like 100,000 flaws. Indeed, by the time Lear says that he is more sinned against than sinning, the very idea that quantities, visible spaces and extents can help anyone understand the play's most prized qualities has been stood on its head. More sinned against than sinning, which for Lear is a comparison shorn of numbers, is this man's first attempt at expressing a feeling, an intensity, that is born of an unpieced whole of experience – the experience of Lear as he is drawn down on fortune's wheel.

* * *

Lear is a prodigal father play, the story of a man who in second childhood wanders into the wilderness, finds humility in distress, and returns to kneel penitently at the foot of his daughter in a classic posture of filial respect (4.6.52). When Lear attempts to bow to Cordelia at their reunion, he is a different man, and king in a different way, than he was when he left Gloucester's castle in a rage. Part of the way the play communicates this change is by shifting our perception of quality itself in precisely the ways that a Bergsonian analysis of perception or motion is designed to do. The play, that is, focuses an audience's attention on what Bergson identifies as 'intensity' by creating situations in which something like pure 'duration' can be apprehended in its qualitative multiplicity rather than its homogeneous order. Unlike *Twelfth Night*, which worked with real and implied spaces in order to create a sense of convergence and immanent interpenetration of spatial domains, *Lear* accomplishes its ends with time, particularly through accelerated or telescoped sequences of action and the repetition of words. The latter strategy doesn't so much negate the perceived reality of place or space – we are not yet in the elastic world of romance and *The Tempest* – as bury huge and consequential differences of meaning within its tiniest interstices. There appears to be *some* kind of meaning to every inch of the play, just as there seems to be some exalted quality of kingliness, different perhaps from moment to moment, in every inch of Lear's frame. Yet that quality, of both the play and character, tends to be most demandingly present in moments where the passage of time has heaped differences of feeling and perception on one another without reference to their compatibility, for example, when Lear suddenly decides to discuss 'the cause of thunder' with the 'noble philosopher' Poor Tom whom he has met in the hinterlands outside of Gloucester's castle (3.4), or when the exhausted king starts praising the paradise of a prison that he will inhabit with his daughter (5.3). Even the verbal line, especially in the scenes that occur outdoors with Lear, tends to acquire its qualities in a spiralling, non-overlapping manner. Everything, in fact, depends upon the gradual accumulation of moments in which verbal patterns – like the 'least syllable' of Kent's 'addition' or curse – merge into new configurations, creating a shifting portrait of the emotional weather on stage. As an image of regal pride metamorphosing into childish repentance and perhaps wisdom, the play always seems to be pointing itself forward, towards broader and more inclusive perceptions, even if forward means passing over the edge of a 'ten mast' high cliff.

The dramaturgical strategy we must now begin to explore is both spatially disorienting and emotionally stunning: inasmuch as the action and words of the play bleed into one another – the sky becoming a portion of Lear's mind; the fool, Kent, Gloucester, and Cordelia speaking to and *for* the king in the old man's nightmare – the intensity of *Lear* the play can shift and turn suddenly, like a flock of starlings that assumes a new form at a moment's notice. This larger interpenetration effect depends on the audience's ability to abandon a sense of time as 'traversible' – as something that can be plotted, measured or manipulated in a mechanical fashion – and instead forced to confront it as something as unpredictable as the weather. What the play must *do* to expose the tragic misrecognition of qualitative modes of being is to lead audiences out into the landscape with the aging king – to draw them into what Bergson would call a space of duration – while partitioning off the punctual political action into a flat, traversable realm of messages and exchanged reports. As a general rule, then, the play presents audiences with two distinct speeds of action, one psychic and qualitative, the other objective and external in its concern with tactics and spatial movements. When Lear is on stage, the former time rules; when Edmund is present, the latter. This contrast, which we will briefly explore, produces moments of dilating apprehension in which intensities of emotion can proliferate and multiply around Lear, with the result that even small repetitions of words and internal pauses in the length of lines become raw and exposed. What we are looking for in the following pages, as we turn to examine the dramaturgical mechanics of the play and the consequences of its revision, is the construction technique that allows Shakespeare and his company to speed up and slow down the action in sudden, jarring ways, a technique which is itself a precondition for the effects produced by repetitions of words and the sudden *retardando* of speech, both of which create a vibrant sense of intensity and qualitative change.

The play's capacity to call attention to what Bergson called 'duration' is related to its ambiguous evocation of space, and I have already mentioned some of the difficulties that this ambiguity creates for spectators of the play. Some of these difficulties are a result of the play's dramaturgy, specifically the way in which audiences are required to infer the locale of off-stage action from on-stage reports of where a character has been or is going, leaving it up to the listener to map that action in his or her mind. As the master plotter or 'artificer' of the play, the bastard Edmund is frequently shown energetically arranging his own and others' movements, whether this is stage-managing the 'escape' of his brother Edgar from Gloucester's castle or shuttling between his two mistresses, Regan and Goneril, in the later acts of the play. The defining quality of Edmund's actions is dispatch, although he does take the time to inform audiences about his plans in soliloquy. At times Edmund may only be on stage for a few moments, as is the case in of scenes 3.5 and 3.7, where he reports to Cornwall on his father's whereabouts and, later, when he arrives just before his father's blinding to be sent by Cornwall to take news of France's arrival to Albany. Edmund's movements from this point on will be extremely complicated: he will travel with Goneril to her husband Albany's castle, but before meeting with the lord will be sent back to Gloucester by Goneril to bolster Cornwall's army. Returning to Gloucester to find Cornwall dead (slain by his servant), Edmund will then be reported by Regan (4.4) to have gone looking for his father; subsequently he will be found in Dover heading up Cornwall's army, caught in between the amorous schemes of his two prospective mistresses and readying the plot for Cordelia's death (she is to be hanged in prison). Around Edmund, who is himself the object of desire and a nodal point of communication for the messenger Oswald, swirl various other transactions, including Goneril's attempt to reach Edmund after he has departed from Gloucester with the message to kill her husband (reported 4.5); Regan's attempt to usurp Goneril's messenger by giving Oswald a separate love token on her own behalf (4.4); and the interception of both the messenger and the letters/ tokens by Edgar (4.5). Alongside these plot developments we have, again, coordinated through messenger, Kent's attempt to contact Cordelia through messenger and tokens (3.1), her arrival related by messenger (only in the First Quarto, scene 17) and their coordinated search for the king, which although successful lands both Lear and Cordelia in the hands of Edmund.

Even Shakespeare's most action-packed history plays, for example the second and third parts of the *Henry VI* sequence, do not try to coordinate this level of interconnected action with implied communications, movements and meetings. Amidst this back and forth which occurs between those who are pursuing and those in flight, we have moments when Lear is on stage – outside castle walls and at times surrounded by a storm in scenes 3.2, 3.4 and 4.6 – where the spatial transactions and tactical manoeuverings give way to introspection. The pace changes, and we begin to hear Lear thinking, and perhaps feel him feeling, at moments when the verse and its inner delays and repetitions become exposed. The process begins with Lear's recognition of the fool's suffering in scene 3.2, where the two men joke about Lear's foolishness in giving away his kingdom. Lear has not yet begun to sound the notes of misogyny that we will hear in act 4, a strand of the play's rhetoric that is as copious and punishing as Kent's railings against Oswald. We get our first glimpse of Lear feeling sympathy in the following lines:

> *Lear.* My wits begin to turn.
> [To Fool] Come on, my boy. How dost, my boy? Art cold?
> I am cold myself.
>
> (3.2.66–68)

'Come on, my boy', is one of the first of several metrically regular five-beat lines composed of single syllable words that Shakespeare uses in order to call attention to the passage of time in the act of speaking. Dramaturgically, the frenzied pace of thought slackens. Lear is speaking slowly because he is seeing something, apprehending something, from a slightly different angle. Feeling or intensity has endured and changed into something else – what Bergson describes as the inevitability of movement and interpenetration in the space of a given duration. The birds have begun to flock another way.

I think Shakespeare began to notice the power of this effect in the theatre and in his revision of the play accentuated it, which is why we see so many manipulations of verbal repetition across the earlier and later versions. He already had the right weather for such changes, so to speak, but wanted to see what happened with the words shifting their movements slightly. When Lear stands outside the shelter in 3.4, he urges his fool to enter the hovel, after which follows a crucial speech in which Lear empathizes with the suffering of others, beginning 'O, I have ta'en / Too little care of this' (3.4.32–33). In the First Quarto version of the play, the dawning recognition seems to flow smoothly from the verse that has been relating his feelings of betrayal and rage towards his daughters. He urges the fool to 'seek thy own ease' and then notes that 'this tempest will not give me leave to ponder / On things would hurt me more; but I'll go in' (Q11.23–24). The First Quarto version of the play follows this metrically regular sequence with the beginning of the empathetic strain: 'Poor naked wretches wheresoe'er you are . . .' (Q11.25). The revision of the play, however, inserts a canter in the middle of the gallop here, as if to prepare for the shift and let us hear the psychic turn as it stretches out in time. Here is the First Folio reading of the passage, with the addition in boldface:

> *Lear.* Prithee, go in thyself. Seek thine own ease.
> This tempest will not give me leave to ponder
> On things would hurt me more; but I'll go in.
> **[To Fool] In boy; go first. [Kneeling] You houseless poverty –**
> **Nay, get thee in. I'll pray, and then I'll sleep.**
> Poor naked wretches, wheresoe'er you are.
>
> (3.4.23–27)

Again we have the monosyllabic line of ten beats (five stresses), not a huge change in the meaning of what Lear has been saying, but a definite slowing, as if Lear must metrically and physically compact himself in preparation for next passage. The delay or added space implied by this change of tempo also allows for the feelings of the surrounding characters, the onlookers, to seep in and colour Lear's emerging regard for the sufferings of others.

The variable speed and interpenetration of thought can also be manipulated through verbal repetition, something that Shakespeare may have been aware of when he was cutting and adding to Lear's repeated words in subsequent scenes. In 3.6, for example, a scene which the First Folio cuts substantially (an entire 'mock trial' of Lear's daughters spanning over 40 lines is removed), even small repetitions are singled out for cutting. As Lear, exhausted from his railing, is being put to bed by Kent, he says:

> *Lear.* Make no noise, make no noise. Draw the curtains. So, so,
> so. We'll go to supper i'th' morning. So, so, so.
>
> (Q13.72–73)

Consider now the quality of the alternative in the Folio:

> *Lear.* Make no noise, make no noise. Draw the curtains. So, so.
> We'll go to supper i'th' morning.
>
> (3.6.37–38)

What is the difference between three so's and two? Between a pair of repetitions and a single occurrence of repeated words? Perhaps none semantically, but there is a difference, in terms of intensity, on stage. Even if actors took repeated terms such as 'so' and 'O' as cues to improvise, it is significant that Shakespeare *imagined* a different consequence following from specific numbers of words spoken aloud. In the revised First Folio version, the curtain closes on Lear's thoughts, ending on a statement. The quality of the last line is that of a musical cadence, with sleep to follow. The repeated 'so's on the other hand, particularly at the end of the line in the First Quarto, pull Lear off into further rumination: so this moment goes, so the next, and so, and so. The metronome effect may have been too powerful at this moment, since the goal of the scene is essentially to remove Lear's consciousness from view rather than show it trailing off in *diminuendo* fashion.

Two of the most dramatic uses of verbal repetition occur after Lear has been taken to Dover by Kent, both occurring in scenes that serve as major points of convergence for the divergent strands of the plot. Scene 4.5, for example, is one of most capacious of the play, accommodating Gloucester's arrival (now blinded) with Edgar at Dover, where Lear wanders in by chance, wearing a crown of flowers. Lear and Gloucester's eventual recognition and the oblique commentary they offer on the nature of suffering prove to be the most expansive, and perhaps also emotionally turbulent, exchanges in the play, giving way almost immediately to more bustle and exchange once Lear has left the stage. Having entertained and ultimately redirected Cordelia's messenger who runs to catch the fleeing king, the group is then encountered by Oswald, whom Edgar kills, enabling the latter to obtain written proof of Edmund's and Goneril's treason. The ferocity of Lear's emotions and the technique of the monosyllabic line are both pushed to extremes in this scene as Lear thinks about the betrayal he has experienced at the hands of his daughters and sons-in-law. The two versions of the play are similar in their rendering of this passage, although First Folio makes an addition (in bold face) that makes the lines more metrically regular:

> *Lear.* [*removing his crown of weeds*] When we are born,
> we cry that we are come
> To this great stage of fools. This' a good block.
> It were a delicate stratagem to shoe
> A troop of horse with felt. **I'll put't in proof,**
> And when I have stol'n upon these sons-in-laws
> Then kill, kill, kill, kill, kill, kill!
>
> (4.5.171–77)

Time stops when Lear slams into the last line, the repetition producing a punishing series of identical verbal blows. He is beating a dead horse, flogging a corpse. And he is breaking the metre that the First Folio is trying to preserve in the process.

Lear's monosyllables are one of the great terrors of the play. They are also one of the great techniques that Shakespeare found for stripping number of its flattened, cumulative meaning and engaging his audience in a type of counting without accumulation. Kill, kill, kill. Even three are enough to destroy the enemy, but with each silent space between the words, the audience will register something particular – and something qualitatively different – at the fourth, the fifth and the sixth. Bergson explains this phenomenon in which numbers acquire emotional or purely qualitative significance with an example from his writing. While composing *Time and Free Will*, he says, he hears the clock begin to strike:

> My inattentive ear does not perceive it until several strokes have made themselves heard. Hence I have not counted them; and yet

I only have to turn my attention backwards to count up the four strokes which have already sounded and add them to those which I hear. If, then, I question myself carefully on what has just taken place, I perceive that the first four sounds had struck my ear and even affected my consciousness, but that the sensations produced by each one of them, instead of being set side by side, had melted into one another in such a way as to give the whole a peculiar quality, to make a kind of musical phrase out of it. In order, then, to estimate retrospectively the number of strokes sounded, I tried to reconstruct this phrase in thought: my imagination made one stroke, then two, then three, and as long as it did not reach the exact number four, my feeling, when consulted, answered that the total effect was qualitatively different. . . . In a word, the number of strokes was perceived as a quality and not a quantity. (127–28).

Bergson's example is fascinating precisely because it helps us understand what the prosodic techniques of metrical regulation, syllabic variation and pure repetition might produce on stage – that is, on the level of the audience's felt response to verse as a dramaturgical element. The flux of duration within the spectator is always working to recoup and synthesize the 'numbers' of lines, beats and syllables, and does so by transposing quantity into quality. The sixth kill kills in ways the fifth does not. Perhaps another analogy for this qualitative or emotional resonance of number might be found in the famous William Carlos Williams poem about the number 5 ('The Great Figure') or the Charles Demuth painting it inspired, 'The Figure Five in Gold'. Both pieces, once seen or heard, change the emotional meaning of the number itself, just as repeated exposure to a five rather than a four beat line in drama can give one the feeling of thought or discourse (five beats) as opposed to incantation or song (four beats).

The most significant changes in repetition, and consequently, the emotional significance of number, occur in the final act, when Lear enters with the dead body of Cordelia. The very fact of Lear's entrance with a body in this scene is crucial to its meaning, since Cordelia's life was one of those vital substances that might have been saved had

Edmund's messenger been dispatched instantly – if there had been no iron law of distance separating the countermand from the prior execution of Edmund's order to hang Lear's daughter in prison. There is an indifference of extended time and space to the desires of those who must traverse them which makes the death of Cordelia seem particularly galling, both to Lear and to the audience. Even more disturbing, perhaps, is the fact that the countermanding order could have been issued earlier – was not dispatch Edmund's great virtue? – had the group begun immediately to think about Lear and his daughter after Edmund's defeat. (Instead, they discuss Edgar's identity and the deaths of the other sisters until Kent arrives to redirect the scene.) By the time Lear arrives with the line 'Howl, howl, howl, howl!' (5.3.231), then, the play is really unfolding in two separate landscapes: a tragic realm of extension in which the physical limits of things, places and objects rule; and a now lost world of intensity where emotions spread, move and envelop their objects with a fluid logic of their own. The defining feature of this latter, durational world, is life, an animating force that, in concert with memory, links the body to its sensory world and allows for consciousness to summon up emotions and feelings with or without subjecting them to the static logic of space. The First Folio version of this scene shows Shakespeare using all of the techniques I have described above to intensify the felt duration of the scene, and thus the meaning of quantity itself which, if it is life, has been reduced to nothing:

> *Lear.* And my poor fool is hanged. No, no, no life?
> Why should a dog, a horse, a rat have life,
> And thou no breath at all? Thoul't come no more.
> Never, never, never, never, never.
> [*To Kent*] Pray you, undo this button. Thank you sir.
> Do you see this? Look on her. Look, her lips.
> Look there, look there. He dies.
>
> (5.3.280–86)

The entire meaning of this last speech hangs on the terrible feeling evoked by the repeated sequence: never, never, never, never, never.

With it the clock strikes five, the iambic metre runs backwards, and the meaning of repetition becomes immeasurable, unspeakable and yet for that very reason ever more emotionally precise.

What has accumulated with Lear's experience? What quality of wisdom or knowledge attaches to his years? Shakespeare is thinking about these questions when he goes to revise these lines – they are perhaps the most pressing questions of the play – but he is also thinking, at that very moment of revision, about the effects of repetition on his audience's ear and verbal memory. The First Quarto version of Lear's final moments is significantly different. First, it prints this scene in prose and thus does not allow the full figure of five beats to govern the lines. More significantly for our purposes, it cuts one of the 'no's in 'No, no, no life' and prints three 'nevers' instead of five. One can speculate about whether Shakespeare wanted the *Lear* that appears in the First Quarto to contain three nevers: the person setting the type on the First Quarto page appears to have been running out of page space in the final scene and so may have truncated some of the text of his original copy (which may have held more). But even if the original version of the play had five nevers and was subsequently altered by a compositor, it appears that Shakespeare was keen to let his audience hear all five in the revised version and, with that quantity of repetition, the entire overtone series of associations – categorical, pitiful, awful, clinical, spiteful – that could have been sounded in a line of blank verse. The old king dies repeating monosyllables, the audience feels time stop in a dilating present: suddenly another life is gone.

* * *

There is respite in *Lear*, but it is offered in prison. The moment in the play when Lear and his daughter dream about a life without cares – when they dream the dream of mutual abdication – is one of the great redemptive turns in the play. Here too we see elements of Shakespeare's meditation on the nature of quality and quantity, this time in the suggestion that the punishing world of this for that – of 'moeties', balances, of greater and less, all the varieties of quantity reckoned and scaled – could be left behind for good. Such a realm of pure quality resembles the space of reverie and pure duration that Bergson argued is the fundamental perceptual basis of life. In it, the world is apprehended as an unfolding rhythm or musical phrase, eddying and collecting in memory while feeling stretches out into a world it already knows. With Edmund, the greedy arranger of worldly business, looking on, Lear answers his daughter's question about whether they will see his other daughters:

> *Lear.* No, no, no, no. Come, let's away to prison.
> We two alone will sing like birds i'th cage.
> When thou dost ask me blessing, I'll kneel down
> And ask of thee forgiveness; so we'll live,
> And pray, and sing, and tell old tales, and laugh
> At gilded butterflies, and hear poor rogues
> Talk of court news, and we'll talk with them too –
> Who loses and who wins; who's in, who's out;
> And take upon 's the mystery of things
> As if we were God's spies; and we'll wear out
> In a walled prison packs and sects of great ones,
> That ebb and flow by th' moon.
>
> (5.3.8–19)

Lear's dream of a prison paradise is impossible, of course; the play will not allow anyone, even someone who is capable of living and suffering so long, to live entirely by the 'ebb and flow' of the moon. What we are given here is a vision of pure duration, of singing birds in a cage who now tell old tales and gossip idly about the rise and fall of courtiers with no interest in measuring their ascents and declines for the purposes of overtopping. Even measures of degree, father over daughter, will be relaxed here as monarch becomes the kneeling son to his own princess. The conductor king has drawn forth the play's most optimistic note, and in doing so has drawn the audience into his own sonic world, one in which words beat the air like the wings of a migratory song.

In attending carefully to the quantities and the process of verbal accumulation on stage, Shakespeare acknowledged the tragic disjuncture between the two realms of quantity and quality that clash in his play. One can count the accumulating years of one's life, even have white hairs, but these are no sure measure of 'ripeness' or of 'wisdom', both of which are crucial *qualities* that *Lear* is continuously working to isolate as such. Similarly, one can assume that the same feeling of despair will be intensified by repeating the word 'never' five times rather than four, but as those words linger in the air, it becomes clear that the feeling itself changes with each repetition. There is a point where the precision of numbers and their variants begin to show their inapplicability, their conjugation of quantity into wholly incomparable feelings. Both Shakespeare and Bergson understood – one from his stage revisions, the other from his meditations on perception – that the realm of quality is a proliferating one: feelings and intensities cannot be divided or multiplied, added to or subtracted from, *without becoming other feelings*. Take away a third of his kingdom and Lear will be a different king. Take away two eyes instead of one and the still-sighted Gloucester will become blind. Yet there are still objects in the world – both the world of *Lear* and of Bergson's study where the clock strikes four. Such objects can manifestly suffer addition and subtraction while remaining themselves. Would Edmund's sword, referred to at the end of the play, cease to be a sword if it were an inch shorter or longer? Does every board cease to be a board when it loses a few inches of its length? Unlike Gloucester and Lear, there is something blind and inert about the obdurate things of the world that cannot be reconciled with the multiplying intensity of consciousness. And if the embodied realm of real distances and negotiated obstacles introduces such a distance or incompatibility into the play or Bergson's world of perception, such a division has consequences for the larger metaphysical position – monist, dualist, pluralist – that we can discern in both the playwright's work and the philosopher's system.

Where, finally, would we place *Lear* in this taxonomy of metaphysical positions? It depends on where we situate intensity, since as a domain of experience it can be identified with the entirety of the play or with some smaller part or region. On first glance, intensity in *Lear* appears to be a fugitive experience: it evaporates in the presence of practical consciousness and yet is terrifyingly dependent, as a quality of life, on the successes and failures of that consciousness. Could Edmund have countermanded the order to execute Cordelia at the crucial moment that he decides to 'do good' instead of asking Albany if he 'had something more to say' (5.3.191–92)? The dependence of life on practical calculation is an integral part of the tragic vision of *Lear*, and one wonders if Bergson, had he chosen to write about tragedy – he did so about comic laughter – would have seen this dependence-in-disjunction of the two domains of experience as the basic tragic predicament. The disjunction is both generic and metaphysical, for what Shakespeare characterizes as the tragic indifference of matter, bodies and landscape to the animating desires of life may also be a philosophical boundary point from which the unity of being, a unity that belongs strictly to the fluid and interpenetrating world of qualities, can only be grasped provisionally or counterfactually. One of the metaphysical choices that the play must ultimately 'make' is that of depicting a world which is either experientially unified or fissured in some categorically irrevocable way. Given our reading of the final tragic necessities, which involve practical calculations of space, elapsed time and risk, *Lear* the play appears to be a permanently divided kingdom, one in which the intensity of the old man's accumulated experience is always opposed to the material props and bodies on stage – bodies that the play suggests can ultimately exist without life. On the level of its plot and articulated values, then, *Lear*'s universe appears to be a dualistic one whose two distinct domains we can explore, but not exhaust, with the opposed terms such as quantity versus quality; intensity versus calculation; durational life versus terminus-bounded death.

Yet on the level of action and dramaturgy, this dualistic separation evaporates, since the stage demands that the embodied actor and an engaged audience collaborate on the creation of a qualitatively rich, durationally saturated world. The dualistic or divided kingdom that Shakespeare explores on the level of theme and plot then *is not divided on the level of practice*, which is where Shakespeare is having his most important metaphysical insights. In the realm of theatrical practice, there is no prison or 'kingdom within the kingdom' in which the pure durational characteristics of life can be sequestered from the alterations of time and movement. All drama uses extension, space and something like an irreversible time (at least on the level of performance) in order to make its action real and communicate it to a similarly arrayed and embodied audience. This embodiment and spatialization is what gives drama its vividness and presence, although it is easy to mistake the nature of the linkage between the two apparently distinct kingdoms of spatial embodiment and durational perception.

The key to reconciling this tension, both in theatrical practice and in the metaphysical system offered by Bergson, is to – once again – avoid spatializing the terms of the analysis. Of course there are bodies on stage and distances in both real and imagined worlds that have to be traversed. And equally, there are calculations that can be made with perceived accumulated quantities, whether one is engaged in counting money, measuring motion or testing the love of one's children. But the basis for these comparisons, according to Bergson, is a process of sensations that is itself in flux. We should not confuse this flux of *sensation* with the stability and extensive solidity of the bodies that are their punctual causes. Thus, when he talks about experiencing a qualitative change in a particular flavour he has enjoyed since childhood, Bergson writes:

> When its changeableness becomes so obvious that I cannot help recognizing it, I abstract this changeableness to give it a name of its own and solidify it in the shape of a taste. But in reality there are neither identical sensations nor multiple tastes: for sensations and tastes seem to me to be *objects* as soon as I isolate and name them, and in the human soul there are only *processes*. What I ought to say is that every sensation is altered by repetition, and

that if it does not seem to me to change from day to day, it is because I perceive it through the object which is its cause, through the word which translates it. (131)

We are returning here to some of the ideas we explored in our discussion of Whitehead: the primary phenomenon to be distinguished in metaphysical analysis – the one that is most easily distorted by our habits of thought, common sense and inherited scientific ideas – is that of change and process. Lear's invocation of music during his final scene with Cordelia is thus a longing gesture towards a primary reality, that of immanence and flux, which *Lear* the drama has been designed to disallow. This universe of process and sensation which *is* performance, one that actually includes the consciousness of the audience member who is counting the beats of the play and synthesizing them in a qualitative form of memory, is the ultimate substance of the theatrical universe. But in *Lear* we are only given clues about the nature, not the number, of this substance. If the construction of the play suggests to us that intensity, or the immanent interpenetration of feeling, is what is really real about *Lear*, our appreciation of that fact will not lead us any closer to an understanding of the substance for which intensity turns out to be the defining attribute.

We must conclude, then, that as a dramaturgical essay into the nature of theatrical experience, *Lear* is only potentially unified by a kind of boundlessness of quality that is as multiple as it is divisible. Such a unity in multiplicity resembles the encircled and encircling sets of actors in the action of *Twelfth Night*, and the higher 'social' unities in Whitehead's metaphysical scheme of ascending levels of solidarity. But this unity must remain potential in the terms of our own analysis of Shakespearean metaphysics. To make such a unity actual would mean showing where intensity is, what it is a feature *of*, and doing so by means of a demonstration of theatrical art. True, the feelings of *Lear* – the flock-like alterations of emotions it stages – are constantly interpenetrating, and they are ultimately the only thing that is left by the end of the play, where Edgar implores all who see the action to 'speak what we feel' in the 'sad time we must obey' (5.3.298–99). But if quality is all that is left in *Lear*, and if Shakespeare's manipulation of pacing and repetition show us that such quality, tone or musical whole is radically immanent to the sequence that produces it, we are still left to wonder whether feeling has a limit or an edge, a beginning point or an end. Is the substance of theatrical experience one or many? A heterogeneous multiplicity or a confused unity? For the answer to these questions, we must turn to Spinoza and *The Tempest*.

Chapter 4

Spinoza and *The Tempest*: An Island of One

There are several obvious senses in which *The Tempest* presents a world that is one. Most conspicuous perhaps is the geographic unity of the play. Because *The Tempest* takes place on an island, both the experience it offers as theatre and the imaginary locale in which the story itself unfolds are subject to an encompassing boundary. The edge of the island, if we are ever allowed to see it, is impassable for most of the characters in the play save Ariel and his minions. Such a limitation appears to have encouraged Shakespeare to honour the classical unities of drama, corralling all of the action within a single location and limiting it within a continuous period of elapsed time which, as several remarks in the play show, spans three to four hours (close to the time of the actual performance). In part because it unifies the action of *The Tempest* in terms of place and time, the edge of the island is also a metaphysical boundary encircling the play, limiting its existence as both an imagined world and a theatrical performance. While there may be a Naples and Tunisia that the characters have visited, these cities are far removed from the action that unfolds on stage. The virtual geography of this world is one in which all locations must pass through the island – be mentioned within its shores – in order to become real. This requirement that events and locales be 'channeled' through the depicted space on stage is as much a function of the limits of performance as it is of the geographical strictures placed on the plot by its island premise. In theatre space, the stage has a centripetal power since the story of an entire world must be told in the limited physical environment of a particular theatre. The requirement also raises questions about what lies 'outside' this bounded space. Exactly where, for example, does *The Tempest* stop and London, *circa* 1611, when the play was performed at the king's Banqueting House in Whitehall, begin? By thinking deliberately in terms of spatial boundaries, we find that the 'shore' of the island world within the play sits on exactly the same geographical lay-line as the metaphysical edge of the theatrical illusion, defining a threshold where theatre stops and something other begins. A play that is all about the limits of theatrical reality and the charmed world that lies within its bounded shores, *The Tempest* offers us an opportunity to think in remarkably precise ways about the metaphysical status of theatrical substance, a substance that the play suggests must by its very nature be a unity of one sort or another.

When classical philosophers thought about the potentially infinite size of the universe, they used to dream of piercing its edge with the tip of a spear. This was something they could never try. As audiences for a performance, playgoers are in a marginally better position to probe the limits of the theatrical universe: they can always throw something on stage, and playwrights can pierce this threshold in a number of ways as well. We have to remember that, despite all of its rhetoric of self-containment and the geographical conceit of isolation, *The Tempest* is performed for an audience used to interacting with actors on stage. Renaissance audiences were ultimately shipwrecked on the same island as the performers they paid to entertain them, and it was not uncommon for playgoers to comment aloud about the performance or for clowns to put talkative playgoers in their places – in effect threatening them with expulsion from the theatrical tropics. Indeed, what one notices right away in thinking about the oneness or unity of the imaginary world of *The Tempest* is that, in performance, this remote isle and its sequestered population actually share a great deal of common space with the audience. This would have been true physically in terms of the actual venue of performance, and in the case of the production that may have taken place at the king's large Banqueting House in Whitehall palace, it may have been impossible to forget that whatever was happening 'on stage' was also happening 'in the king's hall'. But it is even more true of the coordinates of space and time that govern actors and audience: the draining of one hourglass on stage appears to take the same amount of time as it would if the glass were sitting on an audience member's lap. And while there may be a few moments when the literal space between characters is not exactly 'to scale', *The Tempest* seems fairly consistent in mapping the action onto a 'real' extended space on stage: three feet between Miranda and Ferdinand playing chess is roughly the same 'distance' as the three feet that might separate one courtier in the audience from another.

But the most important element that is shared between actors and audience in *The Tempest* is sound, and it is on the sound that swirls around the performance of the play that we are going to concentrate in our closing discussion of Spinoza, *The Tempest*, and the particular form of dramaturgical monism that Shakespeare embraces in this play. While the audience cannot literally join the actors physically in the performance space of the play – cozying up between Ferdinand and Miranda while they play chess in the final scene – they can and do share the ambient noises, music and songs that slip across the boundary of the stage in ways that no philosopher's spear ever could. Sound in the theatre, particularly sound that is not produced by any visible source on stage or a source referenced 'inside' the story, calls attention to the environment of a performance, providing a second shell of awareness for the spectator who is attending to the visual flow of action as it unfolds on stage. Indeed, the ambient quality of sound – its ability to be in all places without being seen in any particular one – provides us with a perfect medium for thinking about the ways in which theatrical experience immerses discrete bits of action (sword-unsheathing, log-carrying, garment-stealing) in ambient surroundings that somehow seem to contain that action (islands, moods, soundscapes, weather). In *The Tempest*, this encapsulating relation between action and environment is brought to the attention of the audience through recurring descriptions of the island's character and powers. As Caliban claims in his partial biography of the place in act 3, the island is 'full of noises, / Sounds, and sweet airs, that give delight and hurt not' (3.2.130–31). Like the island itself, which seems to be the ultimate environment in which the play's action takes place, music is a medium that flows from, within, and around that *imaginary* place into the ambient space of performance proper. If some of the courtiers from Naples and Milan are lulled to sleep by the island's 'solemn music', the audience can hear this music in a way that it cannot feel the hardness of the boards that the sleeping players lie on.

What is distinctive about the dramaturgy of *The Tempest*, particularly its use of music to cue or accompany action and lead characters around the space of the stage, is that it deliberately confuses the distinction between action and environment, the contents of a theatrical fiction and the container that surrounds it. Far from being a flaw in the play, this confusion actually provides a clue about the metaphysical position that Shakespeare is staking out in the course of *The Tempest*. We will need the help of Spinoza to articulate this position, but it can be stated summarily as follows: if we ask where and how an action and its environment might be distinguishable from one perspective, and yet unified from another, we have to answer that both are part of a larger unity that is metaphysically one but internally diversified. We will have to see *The Tempest*, that is, as a monistic universe that is capable of having parts of its contents encapsulated into 'individuals' whose unity is real relative to the other unities they contain, but provisional relative to the larger unities of which they are a part. It will take the remainder of this book to show exactly why this is the position that Shakespeare chose. Having arrived at it by theatrical means, we should not expect him to employ the technique of strict geometric proof that Spinoza employed in the exposition of his ideas in *The Ethics*. But we can, I think, expect that the journey audiences make while passing through *The Tempest* will be similar to the one they make when they, as readers, move through *The Ethics*. For both of these journeys are expected to *do* something to those who make them. The traveller here must learn, as Prospero does, the shortcomings of living in a secluded cell, or more broadly, the real difficulty of dwelling in what we call, perhaps without knowing what the term really means, an environment. Like *The Tempest*, *The Ethics* is an island experience: it is designed to make its reader aware of a compressed web of interconnections and dependencies that, once understood, can be a source of joy, but which unacknowledged serve as a source of sadness and even violence.

To get to the point where dramaturgy and philosophy meet, we have to back up and look at some of the tensions that govern the play. Let us consider initially the action it contains as a story or plot, which is relatively limited in comparison to the complicated zigzag of events we encountered in *Twelfth Night* and *Lear*. Broadly speaking, there are two types of action in *The Tempest*, the first primarily punctual and the second ambient, or what we might call environmental. Prospero is the working representative of the first or punctual form, since he is positioned at the juncture of a great range of occult forces that he has, by virtue of his magic and books, managed to gather together and control. In opposition to this first type of action, we find in *The Tempest* another specifically environmental form of action, which occurs when an ambient entity such as the weather, music or even the bounded space of the island becomes active in its own right, developing a power and personality of its own. Beginning with the first half of this conceptual distinction, we see, in Prospero's ongoing attempts to manage the direction of events on the island, hallmarks of the punctualism discussed in the early sections of this book. Here we discussed the classical and early modern tendency to trace the lines of causal determination back to a particular location in the world, a location which was then endowed with metaphysical significance (an Aristotelian substance, the vectored source of a mechanical force in a body, etc.). This also happens to be the mindset of Prospero who, if we were to diagram the action of the play on a two-dimensional surface, would appear as the hub of a many spoked wheel. Not only does Prospero possess a great reservoir of memories that is crucial to defining Miranda's sense of her own experience, but also his physical ability to manipulate spirits and the phenomena in the environment makes him the principle organizer of experience for the characters and, somewhat less directly, for the audience. All paths on the island, then, would seem to converge on Prospero's cell, although as the plot develops it becomes clear that Prospero is not the omniscient master that he may at first seem. Caliban, who is a native of the island, for example, is well versed in its resources and charms: he knows the meandering paths that lead to the island's sweet springs, paths that Prospero would never have learned without Caliban's aid. Prospero is not, we also notice, himself responsible for bringing the court party into the vicinity of the island. In the first scene with Miranda where he rehearses their joint history, Prospero remarks that it is 'by accident most strange' that 'bountiful Fortune' has brought the old Duke's antagonists into his 'prescient' grasp (1.2.179–81), and that his plans depend upon his courting 'a most auspicious star, whose influence / If now I court not, but omit, my fortunes / Will ever after droop' (1.2.183–85). While he is possessed with considerable powers of action, then, Prospero too is subject to the vagaries of circumstance and occasion that we saw Viola and Edgar cope with in the two previous plays. We need to remember his subtle forms of dependency from the outset, since they will turn out to be a crucial factor in the transition he and play make in the final act.

In opposition to Prospero's magic, which is always a vectored force directed at an object, the island presents a very different principle of action, one that is ambient rather than directed from a point. As Adrian, one of the talkative courtiers, remarks after the noble party's arrival on shore, the island is 'of subtle, tender and delicate temperance' (2.1.43–44), a remark that calls attention to the personality of the island, which seems to manifest itself most obviously on the level of sound and the weather patterns that circle around it. After Gonzalo has regaled his fellow castaways with tales of an immanent republic of 'common nature', the spirit Ariel enters invisibly, playing 'solemn music' (2.1.181). This swirling melody from nowhere has a narcotic effect that prompts the two plotting characters, Sebastian and Antonio, to remark:

> *Seb*. What a strange drowsiness possesses them!
> *Ant*. It is the quality o'th' climate.
> *Seb*. Why,
> Doth it not then our eyelids sink? I find
> Not myself disposed to sleep.
> *Ant*. Nor I; my spirits are nimble.
> They fell together all, as by consent;
> They dropped as by a thunderstroke. What might,
> Worthy Sebastian, O, what might – ? No more! –
> And yet methinks I should see it in thy face.
> What thou shouldst be th'occasion speaks thee, and
> My strong imagination sees a crown
> Dropping upon thy head.
>
> (2.1.195–205)

Antonio's remark reprises some of the ideas we visited in the previous section on *Lear*, suggesting as it does that there is something immanent about the 'quality' that overtakes the rest of his company, like a thunderbolt, dropping two kings and their counsellor into slumber. We can hear echoes of *Twelfth Night* here too, as Antonio suggests that something beyond the power of either individual – what he calls 'occasion' – is actually speaking to Sebastian and prompting him to action, to actually 'be' something new. If we read Antonio's remarks literally, the island itself and its strange qualities appear to have prompted or instructed both men as to what must come next: a crown will 'drop' on the nephew's head, like a hailstone from heaven, if he can only hear what the thunder is prompting him to do.

But the reality of the situation is more complex and here, as elsewhere in *The Tempest*, we see Shakespeare using sound to complicate the action/environment distinction that Antonio is using so deliberately to goad his fellow castaway to murder. For what does the audience see and know at this moment? We have already heard Prospero order Ariel to 'be subject / To no sight but thine and mine, invisible / To every eyeball else' (1.2.304–06). And yet Ariel the actor must arrive punctually on stage here, as the stage direction requires, and play the 'solemn music' that none of the characters will comment on directly. Rather, we only see them affected by this music – and only a portion of them, since Sebastian and Antonio remain awake during their slumber until Ariel returns to whisper a song of danger into Gonzalo's ear. Shakespeare is relying on the audience, then, to imagine that only certain characters are subject to the charm of Ariel's sound, even though everyone in the theatre can hear it and understands something of its strange origins. Our knowledge also tells us that Antonio and Sebastian are not entirely correct in their comments about the island and its encompassing charms. While it is true that the island has its own 'subtleties' (5.1.126), these are under the direction of Prospero, who manipulates spectacles around the island for his own purposes – most obviously, his enterprise of revenging the wrongs done against him by Antonio and his co-conspirator Alonso. What from one perspective, then, appears to be a 'quality' of the environment – a diffused power of affection as mobile and invisible as music – is from another understood to be a localized form of action, a task assigned to one of Prospero's minions who has somehow managed to bring these diffuse forces to heel. Action and environment, that is, become convertible in this scene depending on where one stands and, crucially, *what one hears*. For those who can hear everything – that is, the audience – there is a potentially vast array of subtle interconnections between different elements in the environment, only some of which are relevant to explaining what makes a group of harried men suddenly and simultaneously decide to fall asleep in the middle of the afternoon.

Ariel's charming of the party in scene 2.1 is really only one of a series of stage transactions that exploit the difference between ambient sound and the punctuality of action enacted in a limited visual field. Much more dramatic, in terms of its manipulation of staging and sound sourcing, is the initial entrance of Ariel with Ferdinand in scene 1.2, the scene in which Alonso's son wanders on stage with the spirit while Prospero and Miranda look on. As he will be in the later scene, Ariel is invisible to all on stage save for Prospero, who sees what the audience sees as Ariel sings the famous song – 'Come unto these yellow sands / And then take hands' (2.1.378–79) – to his minions, inviting them to participate in the charm that will draw Ferdinand to the waiting Miranda. The explicit stage direction from the First Folio makes it clear that Shakespeare is aiming for a particular environmental effect when the song is performed on stage. I quote from the Arden edition of the play, which preserves the Folio's stage direction as it was printed:

> Enter Ferdinand[,] and Ariel, invisible, playing and singing.
> *Ariel* [*Sings.*] Come unto these yellow sands,
> and then take hands;
> Curtsied when you have, and kissed
> the wild waves whist;
> Foot it featly here and there,
> And sweet sprites bear
> The burden.
> (*burden dispersedly*)
> *Spirits.* Hark, hark! Bow-wow,
> The watch-dogs bark, bow-wow.
> *Ariel.* Hark hark, I hear,
> The strain of strutting chanticleer
> Cry cock a diddle-dow.
> *Ferd.* Where should this music be? I'th' air or th'earth?
>
> (1.2.376–88)

The italicized instruction '*burden dispersedly*' indicates that the voices in the spirits' refrain – the 'burden' that echoes Ariel's word in the song – are meant to surround the stage from many directions, bounding around the space, perhaps, like a ricocheting bullet of sound.

Although it is not entirely clear from the First Folio's printed directions who was to sing each line of the song, the stage direction 'burden dispersedly' tells us that Shakespeare wanted to exploit the spatial ambiguity of sound in the theatre by multiplying its potential sources. It is even possible that the echo-effect specified here was produced from sources invisible to the audience – for example, a boy actor underneath the stage in the cellarage, behind the stage in the tiring house, or above the stage in a curtained gallery. In addition to accompanying music produced from a hidden musicians gallery, there may also have been opportunities in the Blackfriars theatre to make use of a pipe organ, whose sounds would have circled the hall in a kind of acoustic envelope of sound.

Whatever the specifics of historical performance, it seems clear that sound in this scene is being offered as a model for the environmental personality of the island, not just from Ferdinand's point of view, but from the audience's as well. For if the audible sources of the refrain are hidden from view – dispersed into the ambient space of performance instead of issuing from the mouth of a singer whom the audience and Prospero can see – then the music itself becomes part of the fabric of the world that *both the actors and we are experiencing*. The music, that is, becomes a kind of elemental substance, one whose unity is not that of a specific place or point – not that, even, of a physical body – but more that of a mood or atmosphere encompassing all that can be seen or felt. 'Where should this music be? I'th' air or th'earth?' Ferdinand asks, and it is clear from the question that the music he is hearing is both everywhere and nowhere: it has a unity and personality that defies localization, but is nevertheless real and present to anyone who hears it. Such music, by virtue of its dispersed mode of omnipresence, unifies the space without occupying or subdividing it, as a physical body would. Like the music that Ariel will later play for the drunken characters who sing their round, the ambient music that draws Ferdinand to Miranda is a 'tune . . . played by the picture of Nobody' (3.2.121–22). Just as important, the music that Ferdinand says is 'no mortal business, nor no sound / That the earth owes' (1.2.410–11) has an emotional force that alters the inner dynamics of his passions. When the 'sweet air' creeps by him on the tossing waters, he says, it has a double effect, 'allaying both their [the waters'] fury and my passion' (1.2.396). As what we might call a medium of experience, music is thus the ultimate avenue of 'affection', which in the early modern lexicon refers to desires or emotions that overtake the individual from without. A frictionless species of touch, this and other forms of music in *The Tempest* surround individuals and put them into contact with one another by making them part of a single vibrating membrane or envelope. We can think of emotions or affections as the tempered vibrations that pass through this membrane, some of which are shared by all, others of which are localized in particular characters or groups of characters.

As we try to understand the unity and oneness of *The Tempest* both as an imagined locale and as a theatrical substance with its own metaphysics, music actually shows us how such a substance might hold together. Precisely *what* is it that undergoes change in *The Tempest*, and what are the principles that govern this thing's transformation from one state to the next? If there are a number of ways of thinking about how *The Tempest* might *be* a substance – of thinking its status as metaphysical island – what precise sense do we want to give to that unity, having already dismissed the unity of a physical body or a geometric point as inappropriate models for our theatrical being? The answer that Shakespeare gives to this question, again on the level of theatrical practice, is that *The Tempest* is one in the same way that music is one: it is composed of elements that hold together in a state of modal interrelation, elements whose interactions and emotional shadings must be understood dynamically rather than charted from a single point. Like musical sequences that are composed in the Aeolian or Dorian modes – sequences of half steps and whole steps, which in western music are experienced as the emotionally charged 'minor' and 'major' keys – theatre can acquire an emotional tonality that is a function of the arrangement of its elements into a whole. But the unity of theatre is not formal, like the definition of a triangle (a three-sided figure made up of straight lines). We cannot abstract such a metaphysical unity as we would a set of proportions from a sequence of notes, reducing specific episodes of action to variations on a particular scale. Rather, and this is something that I think Shakespeare was particularly aware of as a practitioner of the stage, the unity of theatrical substance is both immanent and material: it actually resides *in* the physical bodies, sounds and smells of the theatre, but it emerges *around* the interactions of those elements in a kind of personality or pitch portrait that is necessarily 'played by the picture of Nobody'. To the extent that this particular view of the theatre constitutes a Shakespearean doctrine of immanentism, we can see it played out on the level of plot in *The Tempest*, whose axial turn occurs when Prospero decides to become part of the world again – subject to its pains, affections and sympathies – instead of reserving his powers to a point, himself a universe unto himself. But the plot is really a kind of second-level articulation of a truth that Shakespeare has already grasped in his long and productive career as an artist, playwright and professional stager of illusions: that theatre is a device for confusing parts and wholes, actors and environments, and that this confusion is not a trivial side effect of 'impossible fictions', but a basic metaphysical fact of our being.

* * *

Under what conditions does the confusion I have pointed to above become possible? I have chosen the language of parts and wholes, action and environment, to identify this state of metaphysical confluence because only broad terms like these can capture the dynamism of a truly immanent view of substance and the changes it undergoes. Such language is directly applicable to *The Tempest*, I have tried to suggest, because the play itself forces audiences to rethink the nature of an 'environment' in the theatre in provocative ways, giving personality and tonal unity to regions of imaginary space like the island and, potentially, to the spectacle of theatre itself, which as spectacle is constantly undergoing changes from one state of dynamic tension to the next. Everything that I have said so far could probably have been argued using the ideas of the two philosophers we have already encountered, as both Whitehead and Bergson are deeply interested in the immanent nature of change and transformation, with Bergson paying particular attention to the 'qualities' that emerge when we use immanence as a measure of being and phenomena. Yet both *The Tempest* and Spinoza's work, *The Ethics*, introduce a further element in the analysis, which it is now time to confront directly. What does it add to our appreciation of immanence in change to say that the subject of that change, the *what* that undergoes and supports transformations from one state to the next, is itself metaphysically one? What, in other words, does the hypothesis of monism – one substance, diversified by many modes – add to our dynamic view of the relationship between the one and the many, the part and the whole?

For Spinoza, this question is absolutely crucial, and his *Ethics* can be read as one long meditation on the consequences of treating all of being as a single substance. In our survey of this text, as in our analysis of the play above, we must concentrate on the kind of unity that is being attributed to substance, since there are a variety of ways of 'belonging together' that, if used to characterize that unity, might slight or distort its most important features. Like Shakespeare, Spinoza sees the unity of his substance as being both immanent and embodied in material beings: we understand substance not by ignoring the reality of bodies and their passions, but by immersing ourselves in them. Only by reflecting on the dynamic qualities of our physical, desiring being and our interactions with other beings do we gain an adequate idea of our incomplete and dependent position in the totality that Spinoza famously (and quite provocatively) calls 'God, i.e. nature'. Unlike Shakespeare, however, Spinoza uses the philosophical techniques of logical implication and geometric demonstration to lay out his position. These techniques can be characterized, briefly, as follows. A thinker working deductively will use the resources of logical implication in order to show that one idea is already present in another – for example, that the idea of a circle already implies the idea that its diameter is twice the length of its radius. Logical implication is a form of intellectual transport: it allows you to know something new and apparently remote via something you already know and 'have in your head'. Geometrical demonstration is easily paired with logical implication, since it organizes a particular train of thought in such a way that the implication of any conclusion in earlier premises can be traced back to those premises in a methodical way. Geometrical demonstration, that is, helps a reader grasp *how* a larger set of ideas is immanent in an apparently smaller one. By structuring *The Ethics* as an extended geometric demonstration and pivoting his argument on moments of logical implication, Spinoza wants to materialize the 'already there' quality of his long series of conclusions in order to demonstrate the immanence of both bodies and ideas within a single, fully determined and logically coherent substance. His conclusions will at times be counter-intuitive, something Spinoza himself is forced to admit when he writes, 'Here, without any doubt, my readers will be in trouble, and will think of many things that will bring them to a halt' (IIP11S, 123). (I will be referring to specific passages in the *Ethics* using Spinoza's divisions, which are listed by Part, Definition/Axiom/Proposition, Corollary/Scholium/Lemma. Thus, IP20C2 refers to Part I, Proposition 20, Corollary 2; a page number will follow.) If the reader continues, however, he or she will eventually discover what Spinoza is aiming at: an emotionally and intellectually satisfying account of how all elements of existence become necessary from the standpoint of a single infinite being, and further, an explanation of how this necessity can be grasped in its immanence from the partial perspective of an individual, embodied human. That is the destination – the shore on the distance, as it were. I will attempt to point out several landmarks along the way in the discussion that follows.

A striking feature of Spinoza's philosophical treatise is its ambition. By introducing what he thought was a simplification of the system of his predecessor, Renée Descartes, Spinoza felt that his own monistic metaphysics allowed him to solve longstanding problems in fields as widely dispersed as ethics, physics, mechanics, psychology and theology. Descartes, we may remember, was a dualist who argued that there were two types of substance in the world – extended matter and minds – and that these substances were not mutually illuminating, which meant that a study of the one could tell you nothing about the other. Like many philosophers in the seventeenth century, Spinoza had difficulties with the architecture of this system, since the two-substance model created a degree of independence among substances that made it impossible to explain, for example, how a disembodied mind might actually move the body it occupied to accomplish this or that desire. Largely because of his deep immersion in Descartes' system, Spinoza arrived at an alternative: instead of two substances there would be one, and the metaphysically irreconcilable elements of mind and matter would become attributes of this one substance, each now capable of assuming a variety of modes. By collapsing Cartesian mind and matter into a metaphysical unity – a unity of which ideas and extended beings were alternate but parallel expressions – Spinoza would thus eliminate the incompatibility of mind and body that was so problematic in the Cartesian account. Of particular interest in this system would be the notion that substance, while it had an infinite number of attributes, had only two that humans could comprehend (ideas and extension) and that these two attributes were related. While it would never be possible in Spinoza's system to understand from the present state of a particular body some future state of mind – one could not make inferences across attributes – it would nevertheless always be the case that the order connecting states of mind was the same as the order connecting states of bodies. There was thus a single necessity in Spinoza's substance, an order of this-follows-from-that, which might be understood in the realm of ideas as a form of logical implication, and in the realm of bodies as dynamic or motive interaction.

We begin to see how powerful this idea of a parallel necessity is when we turn to Spinoza's account of individuals, which occurs in

Part II of the *Ethics*. One of the major burdens Spinoza faces in arguing for one substance is the apparent difficulty of reconciling the asserted fact of that unity with the apparent existence of individuals – for example, living human beings – whose distinctness from other individuals seems incompatible with the larger vision of a single substance. What defines an individual and in what sense does it belong to the whole of which it is a part? Spinoza answers this question by thinking about what defines an individual body, and his answer is surprising. An individual body should not be thought of as a chunk of matter with a visible edge, but rather an aggregate of other elements (sometimes other individuals, sometimes 'simple bodies') that 'preserve towards each other the same relation of motion and rest' (IIP13C2L5, 129). A human being, for example, is an individual defined by certain characteristic forms of motion and rest, for example the pumping of the heart and the relative stasis of the bones. This ratio or mutual 'relation' is something that we must preserve in order to live, and our capacity to preserve this relationship in the face of other forces that are constantly impinging on our bodies is called our 'conatus' or endeavour, which for Spinoza is the tendency of each thing, in so far as it is considered in itself, to 'persevere in its being' (IIIP6, 171). When conatus is thought through the attribute of extension, it is thought dynamically, so that the boundary of every individual includes that individual's struggle against other individuals whose conative powers either augment or diminish the first individual's motive being. An important consequence of this definition is that the individual so constituted must always be understood through its relationship with its environment, the environment being the remaining portion of extension that does not share its distinctive motions. The environment and its array of powers (other individuals), then, is the other half of the all-important dynamic relationship that makes any individual the thing that it is. Crucially for Spinoza, this interactive relationship is, in a sense, already 'inside' the individual by virtue of the tensions and excitations, which that individual must support as it interacts with environmental powers: this means that the overall power of the individual is not to be understood locally as a kind of point among points, but dynamically as a harmonization or divergence of more or less sympathetic regions of extension in motion.

To this dynamic account of bodies and the motion that individuates them, we must now add a further Spinozan doctrine: that all of these dynamic transactions taking place in the attribute of extension are reflected or expressed in the attribute of ideas, and that the mind of an individual *is* the flux of ideas that correspond to its mobile interactions in the realm of extension. With this ideational compliment of the body's fortunes in place, Spinoza is now ready to account for confusion in the realm of ideas, since just as an individual's body does not fully comprehend the totality of the environment whose powers it works with and against, so too the mind – which is the idea of that body – cannot find within itself all of the ideas that correspond to the future states of its body. The mind will never grasp its future fully, that is, because the idea of that future state is not fully implied or *immanent* in the idea it possesses at any given time in the present. And yet, since implications among ideas and motions among bodies are actually separate expressions of the same reality, Spinoza can make leaps between the physical and the intellectual in ways that Descartes never could. One is pointing to the same structure and reality when one says, on the one hand, that an individual body contains other bodies, and on the other, that a given idea contains other ideas. Both senses of belonging or oneness are necessary because they are parallel expressions of the requirements of a single being, God or Nature, which is the only being that contains all ideas and bodies in an immanent whole.

This is one of the great advantages of Spinozan monism, assuming one accepts his premises: it allows you to keep your discussion of human ideas and bodily states on the same level without *reducing* your sense of the human to either mere physical dynamism or idealistic determinism. The necessity governing bodies flows from the same source as the necessity governing ideas: in sensing the one, you are also 'sensing' the other. But of course, not everyone knows that these two realms or attributes are rigorously parallel, and even if one does, one can never get an exhaustive view of either oneself or of the environment. This is because as individuals, our ideas are inadequate, expressing as they do the partial and jumbled experience of our bodies. Nevertheless, just as the body contains other bodies and all bodies contain elements in common, so too the mind can have the idea of its own incompleteness – a sense, that is, of the environment's participation in its own being – and a sense of what it does already possess as part of its nature (IIP16, 131; IIP29C, 141). To the extent that a given individual finds certain ideas immanent within his or her own mind, present in what is already present, then, Spinoza says that this individual will have adequate ideas: in thinking these adequate ideas, the individual will be affirming his or her nature (i.e. his or her distinguishing modes of motion and parallel intellectual states). To the extent that this individual finds his or her own ideas incomplete, on the other hand – finding, in effect, that they depend on other ideas that the mind does not yet possess – that individual will be passive and so unable to act in a way that expresses and affirms its own nature, considered in itself. Incompleteness and passivity (in the sense of being a patient rather than an agent) are thus the unavoidable consequence of the body's confused immersion in an environment from which it is only relatively distinct, this by virtue of its relative agreement and divergence of motions.

Much of the argumentation in *The Ethics* is dedicated to the task of showing how such a partial, dynamic individual might nevertheless clarify its knowledge of itself and so overcome imperfect ideas or confused perceptions by expanding the powers of the body. For Spinoza, such an expansion means increasing the traffic across the 'threshold' of the individual – exploring further that individual's capacity to affect others and be affected by others in their turn. Such a capacity is always augmented through action, which in the mind involves assenting to propositions that seem immanent to what it already knows (affirming logical implications), and in the body involves the active pursuit of similarly disposed bodies whose needs and rhythms complement our own. This pursuit of such a sympathetic array of complimentary bodies is described in Spinoza's theory of the active and passive emotions or 'affects', which he argues are always oscillating between greater and lesser degrees of conative satisfaction. Satisfaction here is thought of, again in the realm of extension, as the greater or lesser power of preserving one's distinctive ratio of motion and rest. The theory of emotions that results in Part III is one that explains how the same endeavour or conatus that holds an individual together over time is at work in driving that individual towards sources of interaction that increase its distinctiveness (ratio of motion and rest) in the larger environment of extended things. Pleasure, in this context, is the affect that is felt when the endeavouring power of a body increases, whereas pain is the affect that corresponds to any decrease in a body's conative power. Part of what makes Spinoza's work a treatise on ethics is the fact that these satisfactions can be frustrated if the individual encounters or pursues the wrong objects (a result of confusion), which means that to the extent that a body can eventually sense its actual dependence on other bodies and feel its distinctive ratio of motion and rest, it develops an appetite for the even *greater* pleasures that await from having its nature confirmed and sustained in mutually satisfying interactions (3P53, 205; 4P20, 241). (Spinoza's political theory in Part IV offers an account of how the common vitality of individuals is augmented when they bind themselves together in a commonwealth.) From the theory of motion and the dynamic tensions that create bodies and individuals, then, Spinoza moves us through a discussion of the powers of desire and the possibilities of interaction that complete those desires within a dynamic, integrated substance. Individuality is not an illusion in this system, but a characteristic state of motion defined interactively with respect to other individuals in the environment whose desires and affections are vitally connected to our own. The unity of substance, comprehended under the attribute of extension, is like the unity of a vast whirlpool, with certain regions or standing eddies persisting in their being, others disappearing, and still others appearing from the muddle of waters.

Before we discuss the dynamic interchange of individual and environment that is the link between Spinoza's metaphysics and Shakespeare's *Tempest*, we need to clarify two additional points, the first concerning the conative power of ideas, and second about the desired state of happiness or 'blessedness' to which his ethical practice is supposed to lead. We resume with the dynamic conception of body. For all that has been said about Descartes' reduction of the human body to a mere mechanical thing, it must be pointed out his own theory of bodies was just as dynamic as Spinoza's: he too believed that bodies were not defined by borders but by their distinctive relative motions. What makes Spinoza's theory of human being different from Descartes', however, is what he does with ideas. Unlike Descartes, who places the mind over and above this vortex of extension, giving it the voluntary power of changing the direction of the body it inhabits after removing itself into an independent realm of ideas, Spinoza says that the mind is in an absolutely symmetrical sense always the *idea of the body*, the latter (we remember) being defined as a distinctive ratio of motion and rest that strives to expand itself within the confines of its environment. At this point our dynamic system of relatively stable bodies in motion finds its counterpart in the realm of ideas, since the idea that is the human mind also exists in the mind of God (IIP11C, 123). The order and connection of ideas being the same as the order and connection of things, we find that Spinoza's one substance is really the sum of all motions – it is the ultimate ratio of motion and rest within the infinity of extension. Simultaneously, it is the one big idea that includes, as an immanent consequence of its own structure, the infinity of all other ideas (these ideas corresponding to all bodies that exist). We are thus encouraged to take a double perspective on any given individual in the world, no matter how simple or complex, since that individual's nature can be thought either from the standpoint of substance – in which case its utter necessity is assumed, both dynamically and logically – or from the standpoint of that individual itself, in which case only a part of that individual's necessity (the part that we *are*) can be understood and affirmed. Where Spinoza finds the greatest prospect for pleasure and happiness is in an ethical practice that mediates between these two perspectives. We must, he believes, appreciate that our bodies, emotions and thoughts are fully intelligible from the standpoint of the one substance. But instead of trying to inhabit definitively that standpoint, which for Spinoza would amount to taking an impossible object of thought, he encourages us instead to elaborate our own particular perspective on the world and in doing so expand our necessarily limited, but for that very reason intelligible, participation in the immanent order of ideas and bodies.

In such an ethical practice, knowledge of the individual becomes knowledge of the environment and vice versa, since both are involved in the elaboration of a particular being's nature or essence. When we think actively about how we, as embodied individuals, belong to such a dynamic structure, we are uncovering the radical immanence of part to whole, whole to part – grasping, in other words, the fact that our environment is in us and our actions in the same way that we and our actions are in the environment. The distinction here is relative or perspectival, and the active individual will find its essence most fully expressed – its logical necessity and physical endeavour most powerfully augmented – when it makes this oscillating connection between its actions and the environment in which they take effect. The pleasure that Spinoza says comes from being 'part of nature', as he puts it in Book IV (IVP4, 231), is really a pleasure of self discover – discovery of a self *in* an environment – and to the extent that the mind finds its own necessity posited in this immanent order that links action and environment, its own endeavour is increased. Indeed, such a transformation of inadequate ideas to adequate ideas is finally just an expression in the realm of ideas of a parallel transformation that is taking place in the body – a moment in which that body's distinctive powers and motions find further synchrony and compliment in the bodies of those around it. Pleasures breed pleasures, then, and as inadequate ideas are transformed to adequate ones, the individual begins to enjoy – physically and intellectually – a certain self-awareness and perhaps intuition of his or her presence within the immanent whole that Spinoza calls 'God, i.e. Nature'. This intuitive form of knowledge is the last and most difficult form of knowledge to be achieved in Spinoza's ethical system, since it is not an abstract knowledge of logical implication – it's not like knowing something about triangles – but an irresistible apprehension of how our belonging to the whole follows *in fact* from what we already know and feel. 'God, i.e. Nature', the one substance, is the only substance that Spinoza believes must necessarily exist by virtue of its formal nature, and so it is the only substance that can comprehend, by *logical implication*, all of the particular states that are included in its essence. But all other individuals, humans included, cannot make such inferences from their own essences, which is what makes an intuitive grasp of particular belonging so rare and powerful. (For us, all particular things that are not comprehended in our individual essences appear contingent: we suppose that they do not have to exist in the way that they actually do.) Once again it is the experience of immanence that defines the moment of insight for Spinoza – here, our intuition of the necessary existence of our bodies and minds in the one substance. As Spinoza writes in Book V:

> [S]ince the essence of our mind consists in thinking alone, of which the principle and basis is God . . . it becomes evident to us how, and in what way, our mind follows from the divine nature, and continually depends on God in respect of essence and existence. (V36S, 310–11)

The necessary and contingent can thus be seen to merge in intuition, but only because reason has the power to intuit the presence of the whole in the part – because our reason *is* God and Nature's reason, and we can know this as a fact of our existence. 'So in so far as we understand this correctly', he concludes a little bit earlier, 'the endeavor of the better part of us agrees with the order of the whole of Nature' (IVA pp. 32, 286). Such harmony is not the music of transcendence, a Platonic rhapsody that plays as the spirit ascends to the heavens only to leave the body behind. It is rather the harmony of understanding that is only possible in and through reflection on embodied being, an understanding of precisely 'how and why', as Spinoza puts it, our own thoughts and bodies can be said to be part of a substance that comprehends them. What does it mean for a substance to be a unity? It means that parts and wholes, actions and environment, are immanent to one another in a way that radically extends the logic of physical encapsulation and strict logical entailment. It means that substance's encompassing song must be sung to itself, and heard by each part as if it were its own.

* * *

When Ferdinand first meets Miranda and her father, he makes a curious remark about the common language they speak. He is led to Prospero's daughter by a strange music that draws him from the waves, a journey from sea to land that prompts him to ask her if she is a local goddess to whom that music is addressed or, less grandly, a human virgin or 'maid'. When she responds in his own language, Ferdinand declares 'I am the best of them that speak this speech, / Were I but where 'tis spoken' (1.2.433–34). Prospero bristles at the remark, challenging Ferdinand – who believes his father, the King of Naples, to be drowned – to explain his own assertion of superior social rank, asking the young man: 'What wert thou if the King of Naples heard thee?' (1.2.435). Ferdinand now responds by saying that the King of Naples is both speaker and hearer of the words just uttered, and that the very act of hearing himself speak in the voice of the king is a source of pain to him:

> *Ferd.* A single thing, as I am now that wonders
> To hear thee speak of Naples. He does hear me,

And that he does I weep. Myself am Naples,
Who with mine eyes, never since at ebb, beheld
The King my father wrecked.

(1.2.436–39)

Ferdinand's response provides us with an important insight into the metaphysical unity of *The Tempest*, identifying as it does the spatial paradoxes that surround acts of audition and vocalization. For the unity that Ferdinand speaks of when he refers to himself as a 'single thing' is precisely that of a self-hearing, self-affecting being – the kind of thing that, as we will see in a few moments, is also the play and its audience when they are considered as one. Indeed, Ferdinand's response to Prospero asserts that the very act of apprehending his own voice in this way ('He does hear me, / And . . .') is in some algebraic or monosyllabic sense identical with the feeling or affection of grief ('that he does I weep'). From its earliest moments, then, *The Tempest* is working to dramatize the way in which the cardinal ends of a basic dramaturgical axis – namely, action (speaking from a point) and environment (the 'place' into which that action issues or unfolds) – become interchangeable when they are located in a single thing or substance. He hears his father speaking, but the voice is his own. He has left Naples only to become Naples.

The grief or affection that Ferdinand feels here is richly suggestive of the ways in which any individual who acts in the world is, by that very fact, also acted upon – that suffering change is always a compliment of bringing it about. Such reflexivity and affective interconnection is precisely what Spinoza is thinking about when he defines an individual body as a unity of motion whose stability must be measured against an environment that 'pushes back'. Like the dramaturgical creature that Ferdinand *is* at this moment, Spinoza's one substance has parts – the one who is speaking, the one hearing, the individual who strives and the circumambient individuals whose striving must be suffered or accommodated. The relationship between these parts is anything but indifferent and there is a strong sense in which each individual actually possesses a piece of its environment 'within itself' by virtue of its boundary-defining relation to changes in that environment. The analogy, then, between the 'singular thing' that is Ferdinand and the singularity that is a Spinozan individual is grounded in the relationship of immanence that obtains between various parts of the whole. There is not a literal 'edge' that defines Ferdinand, just as there is not a literal edge to a Spinozan body: rather, each is defined by a set of characteristic motions or tensions that it is able to sustain. Taking the analogy one step further, we can say that in *The Tempest*, sound is the dramaturgical equivalent of the physical forces that Spinoza relies on in *The Ethics* to create individuals: it is an avenue of affection and thus relation that holds parts and wholes together in an immanent unity. Such unities are real from the standpoint of their parts: Ferdinand's ear is undoubtedly *there* where his voice is speaking, just as he and Miranda are *there* on the island and *The Tempest* is *there* on stage. (We do not have to point to a physical edge of a body, stage or illusion in order to say that what we are describing exists.) But there is also a crowd pushing in on the individual, a scene in the medium of definition that turns out to be shared. For is it not also the case that Miranda hears Ferdinand speak as well, sympathizing in her characteristic manner with the affections that Ferdinand is himself feeling? Doesn't this sympathy augment or modulate the affection Ferdinand himself feels, creating a second inner ear (local Goddess, maid?) in which the voice of the new king begins to resonate? And what of Alonso, the real and very much living King of Naples, who is at this very moment waylaid in the non-place where Ferdinand's voice cannot be heard?

Voices and sounds resonate everywhere and nowhere in *The Tempest*, and Shakespeare's use of sound in the play suggests that this space is characterized more by states of shared affection than by distances or edges. Our attention is drawn to this sonic mode of interrelation, as I have already suggested above, when hearing and the production of sound become spatially ambiguous. We get a sense of this confusion most immediately when music is employed, as it so frequently is in this play, as a charm or force that seems to envelop individuals from sources that are not entirely obvious (for example, in the dispersed singing of 'burden' earlier in this act). Yet Shakespeare also calls attention to the spatial paradoxes of sound when he selectively decants it on stage, allowing some characters to be addressed by music or voices while others remain insensible to them. An example of this latter dramaturgical technique appears in Ariel's invisible mocking of the clown characters in scene 3.2, where he ventriloquises the voice of Trinculo in order to make Stephano and Caliban think they are being abused by the jester. When Ariel says 'thou liest' during their comic interchanges, it is not clear whether or not Trinculo hears the offending remark, even though he is blamed for making it. (Trinculo eventually moves 'further off' because he believes Stephano to be out of his 'wits and hearing', 3.2.69, 74.) Even more deliberate in its use of selective audition is the next scene in which Ariel accuses Alonso, Sebastian and Antonio of having plotted 'sin' against each other and Prospero, which Ariel does after the illusory banquet – self-accompanied on stage by a 'solemn and strange music' – disappears suddenly with a thunderclap. Here it is Gonzalo and the other morally uncompromised characters, Adrian and Francisco, who are removed from the medium of Ariel's voice and so left to wonder when the other nobles draw their swords in amazement and audibly repent their plots against the old Duke of Milan. Looking on the scene, Gonzalo says, 'Their great guilt, / Like poison given to work a great time after, / Now' gins to bite their spirits' (3.3.104–06). To those who cannot hear Ariel's voice, these acts of renunciation or repentance seem to have no prompt but the inner, imaginary voice of conscience. To those in the audience, however, that source or prompt is clear: Ariel has been instructed to remind the conspirators of their plots and in doing so terrify them to distraction and perhaps a state of remorse. Gonzalo remains still while Alonso runs about shrieking in fear. Bodies on stage have assumed what Spinoza would call a characteristic ratio of motion and rest, and sound is the invisible tympanic membrane that stretches between them. Some parts of this membrane (the innocents) remain untroubled, and in choosing to keep the minds of some characters still, Shakespeare has effectively encapsulated a segment of his on-stage audience and used their auditory exemption as an indicator of their moral identity. But even if it has certain dead spots, the tympanic organism that is stretched across the stage in scene 3.3 is still a single thing. Indeed, it is now difficult to say exactly how that thing is different in kind from another important thing – the audience – which is arrayed around it, and is in some sense within it.

Sound, that infinitely sharp spear, has penetrated the boundary of the illusion and continued to travel into the space where the play is performed, suggesting that the envelope which encircles characters within *The Tempest* does not end at the edge of the stage. When we reflect on the unburdened career of sound in this way, all of the suggestive allegories and illustrations of affection and unity that we have been tracking *within* the play start to travel offshore in exciting ways. For it is not simply the case that *The Tempest* shows us what a metaphysical substance might be like, modelling the properties of immanent participation and dynamic interrelation that can be described in the language of Spinozan monism. Rather, and this is where the audible universe of Shakespeare's island world acquires real emotional and philosophical power, the medium of sonic affection that binds characters to each other and their stage environment *is the very same one* that links spectators to the action that they see and hear unfolding around them. The audience, in fact, may be the ultimate resonator in the substance that is *The Tempest*, since it is we who 'hear' everything on stage and in doing so retain and distinguish those sounds from the ambient soundscape of the venue of performance, whether we are sitting in a Globe-like theatre, a private dinner hall or on a platform in the middle of an urban park. As with the final gathering of *Twelfth Night*, where the metaphysical container of occasion has been extended to include the audience itself, the experience of *The Tempest* is one in which each element of the performance – actor, illusion, audience member and venue – is related and bound together in some sort of immanent unity. The embrace of sound that is so carefully orchestrated in the theatre where this play is staged is thus not simply something to 'think about' when considering how we too are affected by, and resonate emotionally with, events unfolding on stage. Rather, in a strictly Spinozan sense, the little eddies of speaking and hearing, acting and environmental audition that swirl through the play are actually 'individuals' comprehended within larger 'individuals' – here the various configurations of audience members who, like the crowd that watches Ariel's banquet in scene 3.3, coheres into regions of more or less sympathetic affection and so characteristic motion. To think this way about Shakespearean theatre is to approach theatre and its metaphysics in a new way. We forget about seeing ourselves 'mirrored' in the characters on stage and start thinking instead about what it means to be *part* of the theatre.

What a strange creature *The Tempest* is! A single theatrical substance, its physical edges or boundaries are metaphysically trivial when compared with the real dynamic tensions that sustain 'it' among all sorts of beings. To be part of *The Tempest* is to be a region of flux, an area of ongoing feeling defined by its resonance with the sounds, pressures and actions that only apparently occur 'onstage'. We could describe this form of dynamic implication or immanent belonging in strictly Spinozan terms, analysing the ways in which the audience has its characteristic motions or appetites increased or diminished by certain threshold interactions with the play. The story of the experience of *The Tempest* might easily be retold, in fact, as the story of how audiences are encouraged to acknowledge a defining tension between their own being and that of the environment of their experience – or conversely, the tension that exists between the actions they take and the environment they *are* for other beings. But it is more useful, I think, to concentrate on what Shakespeare was trying to do with the philosophy of immanence he was evolving on stage in this play, and to ask just what kind of theatre he wanted to create. Something like a metaphysical position is being consolidated when Shakespeare writes *The Tempest*, a position in which the playwright elevates affection above physical contact or visual presence as the ultimate principle of movement and being in his theatre. What Shakespeare ultimately wanted, I believe, was a conative theatre, an affecting experience of immanence that allowed actors and audiences to participate in a larger flux that was both emotional and cognitive in its powers of transformation. As such, this theatre had the potential to be therapeutic in the same sense in which Spinoza's *Ethics* might be said to be therapeutic: it could offer the individual a glimpse of his or her place in an immanent whole that was neither purely spiritual nor indifferently physical. But this experience of participation and immanent presence was not one in which the world was left behind, its particular quirks and characteristic disappointments giving way to a grand Platonic vision of metaphysical unity. Rather, Shakespeare seems to have placed his philosophical bets on the power of theatre to communicate and intensify our feeling of what Spinoza called the 'particular things' of the embodied world – to engage them as fact, but in their aspect of necessary interconnection. Moving auditors towards such a holistic grasp of particular things by immersing them in states of passion or 'affection' is really the ultimate philosophical goal of a play such as this, even if that goal remains implicit in its dramaturgical operations.

We get a sense of how this emotional dynamic might work in the last act when Prospero is seen giving up his magical powers of punctual action. While Prospero is far from heroic in this scene – what, if anything, does he renounce of his presumptive lordship over the natives of the island? – he is nevertheless shown succumbing to just the sort of 'affection' that subordinates him to the limitations of his kind, which in the play is the limitation of human sympathy. Such transition or movement, of course, is what finally makes him part of the whole in a Spinozan sense. The transition begins when Ariel arrives in scene 5.1 with news of the party of nobles, the most villainous of whom he has been torturing to distraction. In Ariel's story it is Gonzalo, the old dreamer of plenty, who elicits both Prospero's and the audience's affection, something Gonzalo can do because he is himself so obviously moved by the sufferings of his fellow travellers.

Ariel describes Gonzalo's reaction to the strange antics of Alonso, Sebastian and Antonio in the following exchange:

> *Ar.* His tears run down his beard like winter's drops
> From eaves of reeds. Your charm so strongly works 'em
> That if you now beheld them your affections
> Would become tender.
> *Pros.* Dost thou think so, spirit?
> *Ar.* Mine would, sir, were I human.
> *Pros.* And mine shall.

> (5.1.16–20)

Interestingly enough, it is Ariel – the play's conduit for song and sound – who is also the conduit for affection at this crucial transition. Prospero, in making the shift from agent to patient which the affection of sympathy implies, calls attention to the fundamental oddity of Ariel's powers, highlighting the latter's capacity to be a conductor for touch and feeling with only the thinnest body of air. 'Has thou, which art but air, a touch, a feeling / Of their afflictions' (5.1.21–22), he asks, and in doing so raises the question of just what Ariel – and by extension, the entire affecting experience of the drama – really is. Taking our cue from Prospero's ambiguous grammar here, we might say that *The Tempest* is an 'air, a touch, a feeling', which is to say, a medium of action that conducts affection and is, as substance, the sum of those affections. Like Prospero, the audience is invited to participate in that substance, which means experiencing their affections as a defining, affirmative limitation within a larger immanent whole.

This experience peaks in something like a flash of Spinozan intuition, which we remember is the moment in his system when the concrete being of individuals and their dependence on the one substance – 'God, i.e. Nature' – is apprehended as a necessary fact. As Spinoza writes at the end of the *Ethics*,

> For although I have shown generally in Part One that all things (and consequently, the human mind as well) depend upon God

in respect of essence and existence, yet that demonstration – although legitimate and beyond doubt – does not so affect our mind as when it is inferred from the very essence of any particular thing . . . (VP36S, 311).

What Spinoza is saying about the 'affecting' apprehension of the essence of particular things may help us explain Shakespeare's decision, at numerous points in *The Tempest,* to make auditory forms of touch – vibration and sympathy – serve as the medium of particularized feeling and affection. For Shakespeare uses the spatial ambiguity of sound throughout the play to focus the audience's attention on its immediate and particular immersion in the auditory substance of the theatre, a substance that can remain metaphysically one without extending itself across a discrete place or receding into a circumscribed punctual location. What makes that experience a vivid encounter with physically present beings (rather than an abstraction like 'Suffering' or 'Forgiveness') is the element of emotion or passionate affection that is shared by bodies on and off the stage. Prospero sympathizes with the parties that have wronged him in the particular way that only he can, which seems to be through the mediation of Ariel's description of his friend's suffering. Does it really make a difference what *kind* of thing it is that he is sympathizing with or affected by – fact, fiction, actor, music, insubstantial pageant or breathing body – when he takes Gonzalo's 'winter drops' as a substitute for the tears of his enemies? To the extent that affection is being shared within a domain that is metaphysically one here, the question of how influence is divided among various distinct kinds of things or substances no longer matters. What matters are shared changes in affection, these changes being more real than any distinctions we might draw between types of actors within the spectacle, or even between the spectacle itself and the various audiences that witness it from 'without'. It may even be useless, on a literary critical level, to continue to distinguish between the 'material conditions' of the performance and the 'illusion or reality' or 'ideologies' that the play is assumed to generate, since the metaphysical position that underwrites such a distinction – the belief, that is, that the stuff of performance is substantively different from the stuff of mind – is precisely one which the play's action and dramaturgy make redundant.

* * *

The ending of *The Tempest* provides us with a final encounter with the immanence of theatrical substance, illustrating the nearly infinite potential for any theatrical action to 'reach out' affectively into its environment and, in so doing, transform that environment into a source of action for subsequent configurations of the substance itself. A few moments after the exchange above, a 'solemn music' begins to play as Ariel leads the crowd of nobles into the charmed circle that Prospero has drawn on the ground. Once again the island is making music and, held in its spell, Alonso, Sebastian and Antonio are being led before both the audience and the wronged Duke in order repent their 'unnatural' crimes. Their redemption, the recovery of the royal children, and Prospero's reconciliation with Caliban his slave all serve to bring Prospero's punctual reign to an end, clearing the way for his exit from the island and return to Naples. By the time Prospero delivers his parting lines in the Epilogue, then, it would appear that he is finally stepping off the island of illusion to make an actor's plea for the audience's approval. And so he is. But he is also reminding the audience of the very real force of the performance it has just witnessed, a pleasure that must be taken in the actuality of beings in the theatre, regardless of what they are made of. Such conative pleasure turns out to be self-intensifying from the standpoint of any truly immanent theatrical substance, a fact we begin to grasp when we examine Prospero's claim that the audience's pleasure *in* the drama will now become its orienting drive. 'Gentle breath of yours my sails / Must fill', he says before his final exit, 'or else my project fails, / Which was to please' (Ep., 11–13). Now it is the environment of the play – its audience or great ear – that is the actor, sending Prospero off into new regions of a theatrical substance with its approving breath. Yet while he may be trapped 'on this bare island' by the audience's spell, Prospero is not really stranded on the literal boards of the stage, at least not in any punctual or geographic sense. Theatrical substance allows for no true islands of this sort, since it is always composed of individuals that are, in the strictly Spinozan sense, the dynamic and provisional parts of *other individuals*. An actor's speaking body and the wooden planks he stands on are one such dynamic individual, but there are many others – a pair of actors in dialogue in one corner on the stage, or that pair combined with a set of audience members who are busy apprehending the speakers' words in some interested or engaged way. Even an early modern reader who is taken with something he reads in the text of the play might be a momentary stability or eddy in the arrangement. For such dynamically interdependent 'individuals' – which are ultimately stable ratios of motion and rest within the larger flux of substance – action and affection are two equally real sides of the same coin. As Whitehead does when he thinks about the prehensive reach of occasions, we can imagine an infinite number of circles around various elements of theatrical experience in order to illustrate how its specific bundles of movement and rest fit together into some larger whole. In the case of *The Tempest*, those concentric lines of affective force extend out to and back from the audience, their mutual immanence guaranteed by the ambient touch of sound.

It is time to end this meditation on Shakespearean metaphysics, which we will do with a few thoughts on Shakespeare the philosopher. There has been a great deal written in the last few decades about Shakespeare's place in the culture of Elizabethan and Jacobean England, and it is undeniable that his plays participate in that culture in a variety of interested and exacting ways. Yet it is equally true that his plays take apart reality and put it back together again in some of the same ways that philosophers do – that his dramaturgy enacts a criticism of our received sense of what is really real and why it is important. In arguing that Shakespeare was, in his theatrical practice, someone who thought critically about the limits of punctualism and the belief that the sources of order in the world are gifted to individuals of a certain kind or place, I have tried to make him part of a larger tradition that resists these ideas, a tradition that includes such figures as Whitehead, Bergson and Spinoza. The spirit of this investigation has been the spirit of the 'and' in the sense that I have tried to keep open the possibility that Shakespeare is always a number of things at once – commercial artist and philosopher, ideologically motivated human being and abstracted creature of the theatre, entertainer and metaphysician. Given the plurality of individuals that Shakespeare and his company *are* in the Spinozan sense, it may not always be helpful to restrict his potential domains of activity as if he were a scarce substance, subject to overextension. Where there are individuals capable of being affected by something we can call Shakespearean, there is Shakespeare, and this is as true of metaphysics as it is of drama. But I have also been motivated by a desire to look beyond ideas that might be contained 'in' the plays and see instead how what they *do* and *are* actually express certain convictions about reality that might otherwise be described in metaphysical terms. Indeed, in each of these analyses – of occasion in *Twelfth Night*, quality in *Lear* and sound in *The Tempest* – I have tried to argue that what the plays presume to be true for their successful functioning as drama must itself stand as a challenge to the punctualist metaphysics that has attracted the criticisms of philosophers such as Spinoza, Whitehead and Bergson. One conclusion we ought to draw from this study, then, is that theatre is not simply a playground for impossible fictions, but rather a critical site of reflection for those interested in what is really real about the world.

The other conclusion I want to offer here is that Shakespeare's work only opens up as metaphysics when it is placed in a larger tradition of philosophers who assert the immanent rather than transcendent order of events. The appeal of this tradition is its worldliness, which is to say, its reluctance to contain the really real in some numinous mental sphere – as is the case in the Kantian tradition of critical philosophy – or to decant it selectively into certain domains of space, as in the case of Descartes' thinking substances. I have said repeatedly throughout this study that Shakespeare was not a transcendental thinker, that he did not exile the body or its emotional states into some kind of material hinterland. Because he was a thinker of the theatre, Shakespeare was a materialist, but he was an immanent materialist, which means that he found purpose, affect and emotion emerging among the actual set of bodies that walked the stage rather than an ideal system that hovered above them. He may have failed to extend this conviction to all who could have benefited from it – what, for example, would a Shakespearean metaphysics say about the sufferings of Caliban? – but it is clearly a conviction that he explored with relentless intensity in the course of his career. Indeed, in the end, we may not need Shakespeare to be a guiding light or ideological compass when it comes to the consequences of his metaphysical position. By placing him in this tradition of immanentist thought – linking the conative principles of his island drama to the immanent dynamics of Spinozan affection, Whiteheadian prehension or Bergsonian intensity – we pass some of these Shakespearean concerns along to a group of thinkers and theorists who have worked through the basic assumptions of punctualism and looked for alternatives. That tradition has always existed alongside the dominant strains of philosophizing – in the West, it stretches back to the atomistic poetry of Lucretius and continues through the more dynamic moments in Marx's thought – and its adherents have always placed a high premium on the specific qualities of embodied experience, qualities that are real because affection is also really real. Far from a doctrine of pan-emotionalism, Shakespeare's theatrical practice offers us a physics of the theatre that is also a metaphysics of bodies and their actions in an environment that is never indifferent emotionally, causally, politically or ethically. This metaphysics is an important contribution to the larger tradition even if a domineering figure such as Prospero cannot ultimately be its spokesman. Others can speak in his place.

Who would those others be? An obvious choice might be Spinoza, who more than any other philosopher mentioned in this book seems to want to understand the nature of illusion, emotion, conflict and politics in a way that acknowledges the fundamental reality of each of these domains. Spinoza's interest in precisely how one might make the transition from superstition or megalomania to something like wisdom – the former being maladies that *The Tempest* associates with Caliban and his co-conspirators in the farcical sections of the play – bears all the marks of circumspection that one might expect from a man who lived through extended periods of religious persecution and political dispossession. A more provocative candidate for spokesman for this tradition might be found, however, in the person of Caliban, the native of Prospero's island who is finally acknowledged by the old Duke only to be dismissed to the duties of 'trimming' his cell. Caliban is many things in *The Tempest* – island-guide, elemental companion of the earth, lover of music and sweet liquors, student, slave and potential father of another generation – but his 'enlightenment' at the end of the play is presented rather monotonously as a transition from savage or infantile credulity to adult wisdom and sobriety. 'What a thrice-double ass /Was I to take this drunkard for a god' he says as he leaves the stage, promising to be 'wise hereafter' (5.1.298–300). Shakespeare will not tell us what Caliban does with this wisdom, and perhaps the omission is fortunate, since within the confines of the play Caliban could probably only repeat the story of *The Tempest* again, recalling his trials at the hands of 'false gods' and affirming the bland colonial order that takes root at the end of the play. Thinking outside the confines of the play, however, we may be able to imagine a scene in which Caliban ends up with more to say about the metaphysical themes of *The Tempest* than his magically inclined master. Let us imagine such a scene now.

Prospero has drowned his books and returned to Milan, the tradewinds of applause blowing in his sails. Many years have passed since the old Duke's departure: his cell stands abandoned now that the island's oldest inhabitant – a philosopher named Caliban – has moved his lodgings to a camp by the sea. Only one book remains on the island, a twine-bound sheaf of papers that the philosopher thumbs through as he sits by the water's edge, listening as he does so to the island's sweet airs and noises. Written in an angular script that is his own, Caliban's book tells a story of superstition, dispossession and the pleasures that can be taken or lost in an island Republic that has no natural master. The title on its cover is *The Ethics*, and its contents is a yet untried metaphysics for a world to come.

Bibliographical Note and Further Reading

In this book I have mentioned critics of Shakespeare's plays as well as texts of the plays themselves and editions of the philosophical works I have been discussing. Those interested in the sources of these quotations and studies can consult the following works:

Bergson, H. (2001), *Time and Free Will: An Essay on the Data of Immediate Consciousness,* F. L. Pogson (trans). Mineola, New York: Dover Publications.

Jones, J. (1995), *Shakespeare at Work.* Oxford: Clarendon Press.

Shakespeare, W. (1997), *The Norton Complete Works of Shakespeare,* S. Greenblatt, W. Cohen, K. E. Maus, and J. Howard (eds). New York: W. W. Norton & Co. (Unless otherwise noted, all references to works of Shakespeare are to this edition.)

— (2001), *The Tempest (The Arden Shakespeare),* V. M. Vaughan and A. T. Vaughan (eds), London: Thomson Learning.

Spinoza, B. (2000), *The Ethics,* G. H. R. Parkinson (trans. / ed.), Oxford: Oxford University Press.

Whitehead, A. N. (1938), *Modes of Thought.* Cambridge: Cambridge University Press.

— (1964), *Adventures in Ideas.* Cambridge. Cambridge University Press.

— (1978), *Process and Reality (Corrected Edition),* D. R. Griffin and D. W. Sherbourne (eds), New York: Free Press.

— (1997), *Science and the Modern World.* New York: Free Press.

Readers interested in learning more about specific topics mentioned in the book may also wish to consult the following:

Deleuze, G. (1988), *Spinoza: Practical Philosophy,* R. Hurley (trans.). San Francisco: City Lights Books. A brief introduction to Spinoza by an influential interpreter of the idea of 'immanence' in the philosophies of Spinoza, Bergson and Whitehead.

Garber, D. (2006), 'Physics and foundations', in K. Park and L. Daston (eds), *The Cambridge History of Science (volume 3)*. Cambridge: Cambridge University Press. An introduction to the early modern philosophy of mechanism in the context of the Aristotelian system it replaced, written by a noted Descartes scholar.

Ginzburg, C. (1980), *The Cheese and the Worms: The Cosmos of a Sixteenth-Century Miller*, J. Tedeschi and A. Tedeschi (trans.). London: Routledge. An intriguing study of an early modern miller who expounded an unusual metaphysical vision under examination by church authorities.

Guerlac, S. (2006), *Thinking in Time: An Introduction to Henri Bergson*. Ithaca: Cornell University Press. An excellent introduction to Bergson and his recent interpreters, particularly noteworthy for offering alternatives to Deleuze's influential interpretation of Bergson's works.

Gurr, A. and Ichikawa, M. (2000), *Staging in Shakespeare's Theatres*. Oxford: Oxford University Press. An authoritative study of period staging with useful information about the positioning of musicians in the theatre.

Hodges, C. W. (1999), *Enter the Whole Army: A Pictorial Study of Shakespearean Staging, 1576–1616*. Cambridge: Cambridge University Press. A vivid set of informed speculations on the staging techniques employed by Shakespeare's company in the performance of his plays.

Lindley, D. (2006), *Shakespeare and Music (Arden Critical Companions)*. London: Thomson Learning. A comprehensive study of music in Shakespeare's plays and the staging techniques that would have informed its use in performance.

Lloyd, G. (1994), *Part of Nature: Self-Knowledge in Spinoza's Ethics*. Ithaca: Cornell University Press. An elegant study of the *Ethics* that makes clear the links between Spinoza's mechanical treatment of conatus and his account of self-knowledge.

Mullarkey, J. (2006), *Post-Continental Philosophy: An Outline*. London: Continuum Press. A comparative study of recent philosophers of imma-nence (Gilles Deleuze, Alain Baidou, Michel Henri and François Laruelle) and the significance of diagrams as an immanent mode of relation.

Nobo, J. L. (1986), *Whitehead's Metaphysics of Extension and Solidarity*. Albany: State University of New York Press. A systematic study of the tension in Whitehead's metaphysics between the singularity of actual occasions and their mutual solidarity, with emphasis on the role of the extensive continuum.

Rapp, F. and Wiehl, R. (eds) (1990), *Whitehead's Metaphysics of Creativity.* Albany: State University of New York Press. A useful set of recent articles on Whitehead's metaphysics, keyed to recent concerns in Continental philosophy.

Rotman, B. (1987), *Signifying Nothing: The Semiotics of Zero.* Basingstoke: Macmillan. A fascinating analysis of the importance of quantity and its link to commodification in *Lear*, offered as part of a larger meditation on the semiotics of mathematics.

Sherbourne, D. W. (1981), *A Key to Whitehead's Process and Reality.* Chicago: University of Chicago Press. Selections from *Process and Reality* helpfully re-arranged into topics with commentary.

Taylor, G. and Warren, M. (1983), *The Division of Kingdoms: Shakespeare's Two Versions of* King Lear. Oxford: Oxford University Press. An important collection of essays on the differences between the printed versions of *Lear*, two of which advocate his role as the reviser of the play that appeared in the First Folio of 1623.

Thomas, K. (1976), 'Age and authority in early modern England'. *Proceedings of the British Academy* 62, 205–48. An overview of early modern ways of reckoning biological and social age.

Witmore, M. (2001), *Culture of Accidents: Unexpected Knowledges in Early Modern England.* Stanford: Stanford University Press. A study of accident and occasion in scholastic and Reformation theology, Shakespearean drama and Baconian experimentalism.

Index

accident
  as falling together of
    circumstances 33
  as novel intersection of plot
    lines 52, 58
  as plot device 9, 32, 59, 95
  in relation to fortune, chance
    and occasion 32, 95. *See also*
    fortune, occasion
action
  ambient modes of 29
  coordinated by report in *Lear* 76
  as dissolving dualist split 86
  of the environment 43
  as immanent analysis of
    metaphysical categories 7–8,
    56
  inclusive of prior action 40
  indistinguishable from
    environment in *The
    Tempest* 92–3, 96, 113
  imagined versus real 11
  magic as 95
  punctual versus
    environmental 94–5, 97
  Shakespeare's interest in 10
  speeds of 74–5
  and Spinoza's conception of the
    individual 107
  taken by part of a single
    substance 26–7

  in theatre, ontologically basic
    nature of 2
  in theatre, reflexivity of 27
  words opposed to 10
actor
  bypassed by action 52
  as collaborator with occasion 35,
    58–9
  as locus of events or activity
    26
  as part of larger Spinozan
    individual 122
  sharing qualities with
    audience 91–2
  taking cues from scripted
    dialogue 79
actual occasions
  as bearing the scars of their
    birth 48, 55
  societies of 48–7, 58
  Whitehead's theory of 18,
    45–6. *See also* Whitehead,
    occasion
actualities, Whitehead's theory
  of 45. *See also* Whitehead
Adventures in Ideas (Whitehead)
  58
affection
  immersion in 30, 119–20
  as integral to dynamic
    materialism 124